DON'T FORGET TO WRITE

Don't

ART BUCHWALD

Forget To Write

ILLUSTRATIONS BY *Laszlo Matulay*

Forum Books 

THE WORLD PUBLISHING COMPANY

CLEVELAND AND NEW YORK

A FORUM BOOK

Published by The World Publishing Company
2231 West 110th Street, Cleveland 2, Ohio

Second printing June 1964

Cover illustration by Jacques Charmoz

Library of Congress Catalog Card Number: 60-11450
Printed in the United States of America. 2WP664

Contents

"Who Needs No Introduction"

THE publisher of this book says I need an introduction. I don't agree with him, but I leave all matters of content, taste, morals, and introductions to him. He, in turn, leaves all questions of sales, advertising, promotion, and print orders to me. It's a very unique arrangement and one that has worked so far. If the book doesn't sell, I have only myself to blame.

The best method of introducing a book is to get some famous person such as James Thurber or Former President Harry Truman to write an introduction for you. If you can get somebody like that, then the publisher can put on the cover

Don't Forget to Write

by Art Buchwald

WITH AN INTRODUCTION BY JAMES THURBER

A lot of nearsighted people will think that James Thurber wrote the book and plunk down their money before they read the small print. It's the ideal situation, but James Thurber and Harry Truman are wise to it now and are writing their own books instead.

I guess the purpose of an introduction to a book is to tell the reader what to expect. "This is a book about etc., etc., etc." It should hook the reader so, when he's browsing through it in a bookstore, he'll immediately want to buy it.

If this is the purpose of an introduction then all I can say—

"This is a book about a woman who loved too many men but with her body and not her heart. Desire, passion, and pain rule the life of our heroine who sought to find happiness at the expense of others. The town whispered about her, but even their whispers were mild to what she *really* had done. Sultry, ruby-lipped, fair-breasted, she drove men mad, mad, mad."

This book has nothing to do with the above. I wish it did.

If you're curious, this is a collection of pieces I wrote on somebody else's expense account. They have to do mostly with Europe where I am based as a columnist for the New York *Herald Tribune*. I live in Paris with my wife and three children who are under strict orders to provide me with at least two of the four columns I write each week. The last three kids I had were busts as far as material went, so I had to fire them. My wife is still on a trial basis.

I am thirty-four years old, and have lived in Europe for the last twelve years. I came on the G.I. Bill of Rights in 1948 against the wishes of my father who wanted me to go into the curtain business with him. I should have listened to him, as the business is doing very well.

Just before leaving for Europe in 1948 my father took me to the boat, and as the gangplank was being pulled up he shouted to me: "Don't forget to write."

Even at the time I thought to myself, "What a helluva title for a book."

1. “What’s Nous”

The Seven-Year Itch

Last year my wife and I celebrated our seventh wedding anniversary. I'm not bragging. As a matter of fact it was a very disturbing thing. When I looked around I discovered that so many of my friends who were married around the same time were either separated or divorced. There were so few who were still happily married that I decided there was something wrong with us.

"We're sick," I said to my wife. "What's happened to us?"

She agreed. "We're abnormal. Everyone is talking. Most of the girls I went to school with have been married at least twice."

"For the last seven years we've been drifting together," I said. "I think we need some outside help."

"I was going to say the same thing," she said. "I'm willing to seek it out if you are."

"I'm willing if you are," I said.

It was good to clear the air and we immediately made an appointment with a divorce counselor.

A divorce counselor operates like a marriage counselor, except, instead of trying to get people together, he tries to break them apart. Most people go to a divorce counselor only as a last resort—when it looks like the marriage is going to last forever.

We arrived at his office together. This was our first mistake. The receptionist asked us to enter separately.

The reception room was simply furnished, with chairs and a low table with magazines featuring stories such as "Wedding Bells Drove Me Mad," "My Secretary Made a Better Wife Than My Wife Made a Secretary," and "How I Invested My Alimony and Made a Million Dollars."

On one wall were pictures of men, and on the opposite wall were pictures of women, whose marriages the divorce counselor had managed to break up.

The counselor came out and nodded to us to come in. We sat down, and the first thing he said was, "I'd appreciate it if you didn't hold hands in this office."

We both put our hands on our laps.

"Now tell me your story from beginning to end, and don't leave out any details. The smallest thing that may seem unimportant to you could shed a great deal of light on the case for me."

We told him everything: how we had met, about our home, how, although we had occasional fights, we always made up.

He kept tapping his pencil against his ear.

"Do you have any arguments about money?" he asked.

"No," I said, "I give it to her and she spends it."

He frowned.

"Now, when you have a fight, does she ever threaten to go home to her mother?"

My wife replied, "My mother lives in Pennsylvania. It's too far to go home, and besides, the children are in school and I hate to have them miss a term."

"Do you ever send your wife flowers?"

"All the time," I replied. "I go down to Les Halles and get them wholesale."

"Does he notice when you go to the hairdresser or when you buy a new dress or hat?"

My wife said, "Oh, yes. I can't buy anything new without him commenting on it."

"What does he say?"

"He wants to know how much it costs."

"And then when you tell him does he get mad?" the counselor asked hopefully.

"No, he just shrugs his shoulders and walks into another room."

The counselor broke his pencil in half. "Do you have things in common to talk about?"

I said, "Lots of things."

"Like what?"

"All our friends breaking up."

"What about your girl friends?" he said to my wife. "Do they ever call you up and tell you they saw your husband having lunch with a beautiful girl?"

"Oh, yes," my wife said. "But that's his job. If he didn't talk to beautiful women at lunch, I wouldn't be able to buy any new clothes."

The counselor threw the broken pencil across the room. "This is the most hopeless case I've ever tackled. Why don't both of you grow down? Everything you've told me makes no sense at all. You have too much in common. You should have gotten married when you were both younger and didn't know what you were doing. If it had only been a war marriage, I think I could have helped."

"You mean it's too late?"

"It's never too late to get a divorce," he said, "but you have to want it. My advice to both of you is as follows: Go home and try to get on each other's nerves. You must be a jealous wife," he said to my wife, "and you have to show a little more immaturity," he said to me. "Keep track of each other's faults. Blow up little things until they seem like big problems. Move into smaller quarters; infringe on each other's thoughts." He lectured us sternly. "Remember this—love and happiness aren't everything."

I thanked him profusely as he escorted us to the door. But when I opened the door for my wife he blew up.

"For heaven's sake," he screamed, "you're not even out of my office and you're already opening doors for her. How are you ever going to break up if you keep doing stupid things like that?"

The Last Film

I WENT to the opening of *Ben Hur* in London, and as they say in England, it was smashing. The press gave it FOUR CHARIOTS, the highest honor any spectacular can rate. The jeweled and black-tie audience were enthusiastic and everyone I know liked the picture, except my wife.

Of course she didn't see it, so she was less influenced by the film than most people. This is what happened.

When I announced that I had received orders to report to the Empire Theatre in London for the première of *Ben Hur* she started crying. "It's so soon," she cried. "You've hardly come back from *The Ten Commandments*, and now you have to leave again."

I tried to comfort her. "A movie critic's life isn't an easy one these days," I said. "I know I'm never home any more, but it's my job. Someone has to cover them."

"Yes," she said, "but why does it have to be you? Why can't they send young men, men without families, men who have the time to sit through the films? The children don't even know their father any more."

"You're being melodramatic," I said. "It isn't that bad. Besides, I hear it's a good picture."

"Sure," she replied, "*Gone With the Wind* was a good picture also, but I didn't see you for four years. It's fine to be a movie critic, but have you ever wondered what it was like to be a movie critic's wife—to sit at home never knowing where her husband is or what's happening to him? Do you know what it is to say good night to the children night after night and see the look in their eyes when they ask, 'When is Daddy coming home?' And all you can reply is 'Hush, children, your father has gone to see *Giant* and he won't return for another year.' Why don't you think of your family once in a while?"

"But, honey," I protested. "You knew when you married me what a movie critic's life was like. Oh, I know you were taken with the glamour of it all—the uniform and the free passes and shaking hands with movie stars.

"But there's more to being a movie critic than that. There's the long nights of loneliness, sitting in the balcony, staring at a curved screen, fighting waves of stereophonic sound, and most of all, thinking of you.

"But this is my life. I wasn't made to stay at home by the

hearth. My father saw the first *Ben Hur*, my Uncle Oscar reviewed *Birth of a Nation*, my Uncle Phil sat through *The King of Kings*. We're a movie-faring family. It's in our blood. And someday, I hope, our son will follow in my footsteps. Someday it is my dream that he will take my place on the aisle in the fourteenth row of Loew's State and review *Son of Ben Hur*."

"Over my dead body," my wife said. "Our son is going to have a normal life. He's going to know what it is to have a family and friends. He's going to know what it is to see the sun and the trees and green grass. No son of ours is going to spend his life eating popcorn in the dark." She started to cry again.

"All right," I said, "I'll give it up. *Ben Hur* will be the last film I cover. I'll hand in my resignation as soon as I come back."

"You're just saying it to make me stop crying. You said you'd give it up after *Diary of Anne Frank*."

"No, this time I mean it. Maybe I won't even stay for the chariot race. I could be back at the latest by July. I'll leave at the intermission."

"If you really mean it—" she said, drying her tears, "if you really mean it—that this is the last time—you can stay for the chariot race."

"But that will mean I won't be home until Thanksgiving," I said.

"Yes," she said, "but you'll be home for good. I want you to get it out of your system. If you didn't see the chariot race you would never forgive me. I'd rather you be home for Thanksgiving and had seen the entire film, than home in July only half a man."

The parting was a tearful one. The children were clutching their mother's skirt. I kissed them each fondly.

My wife gave me a hamper of food. "Where should we send your mail?"

"The Empire Theater," I said. "They'll forward it to my seat."

How To Get Your Heater Fixed

LAST winter the hot-water heater in our house broke. Now only people who have lived in France can understand what this means. My wife, one of the coolest cucumbers that ever grew in western Pennsylvania, loses all control of herself when something like this happens, and it is only my comforting presence which prevents her from packing her bags and taking the next jet to America.

When the event occurred on Saturday morning, I saw no reason to panic. It was an electric hot-water heater, and since we were getting cold water, it was obviously a job for an electrician. I called the electrician and told him the electric hot-water heater was on the blink.

He listened sympathetically and then said that since it was a water heater, it was a job for the plumber. I called the plumber, and when I said it was an *electric* hot-water heater, he advised me to call the electrician. I told him I had called him and had been advised to call the plumber. He replied that the electrician was just passing the buck and there was no sense in his coming, as it was out of his jurisdiction. Even if it was in his jurisdiction, which he once again assured me it wasn't, he told me he would not be able to come until March 1962.

I called another electrician, but this time I didn't tell him what was broken. He said he could come sometime in February. I told him it was a matter of life and death and there was a chance of the whole house burning up if he didn't send someone right away. The electrician said he couldn't come, but would send one of his workers. If it was really true that it was a matter of life and death, he himself would come at the end of January.

I spent the rest of the day hiding my wife's valises so she wouldn't leave. Around six in the evening the electrician's helper appeared.

He was a short man, dressed in greasy khaki shirt and pants, and seemed annoyed at having to make a call so late on Saturday evening.

Before bringing up the problem I offered him a glass of wine, which he accepted gratefully. We talked about the Fifth Republic, soccer results, cycling, and the third race at the Auteuil race track. My wife, who was twisting her handkerchief nervously, couldn't stand the suspense.

"Tell him," she cried.

This broke the friendly atmosphere and the man remembered he was on a job and became surly again. There was nothing to do but take him into the room with the heater.

He took one look at the heater and said, "Call the plumber."

"He told me to call you. Just look at it. I don't expect you to fix it. I just thought you would be interested in seeing a broken hot-water heater."

The man studied it carefully. "Your counter is broken.

It's a hundred years old. So is the boiler. The situation is impossible. You would have to tear out every wire in the house and even then it is doubtful that anything could be done. Impossible! Impossible! There is nothing to be done."

"You are so right," I said. "I was foolish to call you. We're idiots to have thought anything can be done. It's hopeless, absolutely hopeless and I should have known it all the time. You have never been more right."

"But," the man protested, "it has to be fixed."

"No man could fix that boiler," I said. "It's no good."

"I could fix it," he said indignantly. "I can fix anything."

"I beg to differ with you in your own country," I said, "but you couldn't fix *that* boiler, not in a million years."

"There has never been an electric boiler that I could not fix," he shouted. "I have fixed boilers twice as bad as this one."

"Monsieur, I am not one to challenge the word of a man I do not know, but in this case I am afraid you overestimate your talents."

The little man was enraged. "I will come tomorrow and I will show you if I can fix that heater or not."

"Tomorrow is Sunday."

"It doesn't matter. I will be here and you will see who knows about electric heaters."

"No," I said. "You would just be wasting your time."

My wife, who had caught on to the game, said: "Let him try, if he thinks he can fix it."

I reluctantly agreed to let him come on Sunday, and in a half-hour he had the heater working in perfect order. I gave him a glass of wine and apologized for doubting his word.

Flushed with victory, he said it wasn't our fault. After all, in America, he said, when an electric heater breaks we throw it away, but in France one has to know how to fix them.

He left a happy man, and I felt rather pleased with everything. It's rare that an American can bring so much happiness into the life of a French worker.

Les Nouveaux Pauvres

(All persons mentioned in this article are fictional, including the author—for obvious reasons.)

When General Charles De Gaulle announced that the key word to the Fifth Republic would be austerity forty million Frenchmen shuddered. When he said prices would rise but wages would have to remain the same, the citizenry froze, and when he announced that serious efforts would be made to collect French taxes, everyone started calling for the Sixth Republic.

One of the methods of keeping tabs on tax evaders is by evaluating a person's standard of living. It is known laughingly as the exterior-signs-of-wealth system. Persons considered to be living above their incomes can be taxed according to the number of rooms in their villas, the number of feet to their yachts, and, in the case of men, the type of women who are keeping house for them on the side.

In France it is no longer a question of keeping up with the Joneses (or the Duponts), but of getting behind them as fast as one possibly can.

As an American living in Paris, I pay French taxes, so General De Gaulle's edict also had a sobering effect on me.

The first thing I did was to call a regular emergency meeting of the entire family to lay down the law.

"Family," I said, "General De Gaulle has decreed we are all living above our means—something I have been telling your mother for years. The tax collector can now tax us on our standard of living and we're going to have to cut down on any exterior signs of wealth."

"What are you trying to tell us, Father?" said Joel, my six-year-old, who was poking his sister with a gold toothpick.

"I'm trying to tell you that we are going into a period of austerity. We must wipe out any traces of our former life of grandeur. We must look poor, act poor, and be poor."

"Are you asking us to become Communists?" the nurse demanded.

"No, but at the same time we don't have to flout our wealth in public. If we do, the tax-collector will flout us, and it will be a flouting shame for everybody."

"How will this affect the individual?" the cook wanted to know.

"I've drawn up a program for the start. We will add to it as we go along. I will accept suggestions from everybody, but the final decision will be mine."

"Hear! hear!" cried Jennifer, our four-year-old.

"From now on we will hang our laundry out of the front windows of the apartment instead of the back. I've arranged with the concierge to leave garbage-cans out in front of the house at all times, and the children may finger-paint on the outside walls to their hearts' content. I want this place turned into a tenement overnight."

"I wish to protest," my wife said. But the children shouted her down.

"Naturally, I've sold the car," I said, "but we must also trade in Jennifer's English stroller for a broken French model without chrome."

"Without chrome?" the nurse said, horrified. "How can I take her to the Parc Monceau without chrome on her stroller?"

"I'm glad you brought that up. You cannot take her to the Parc Monceau any more. As you know, the Parc Monceau is the playground of all the rich kids of Paris. The tax-collectors are going to be watching every sand pile in the area."

"When can I take my sailboat to the Tuileries?" Joel asked.

"You can't take your sailboat there any more. Sailboats are exterior signs of wealth. You may sail matchboxes or planks of wood, but no sailboats."

"What about my bicycle?" Jennifer, the four-year-old, asked.

"You may use it if you remove the white sidewall tires."

"I suppose this means I can't buy any new clothes?" my wife asked.

"Of course you can't. I've already taken the liberty of slashing the dresses in your closet. We're dead ducks if you're seen on the street in a good dress."

"This is going too far. I'd rather pay the taxes."

"Enough of that kind of crazy talk. If we started paying taxes, our French friends would never forgive us. But the picture is not all black. People are starting to give clothes parties. You'll wear slacks and a sweater to somebody's house and carry your gown in a suitcase. Once inside the house you can change into your latest creation."

"It sounds ghastly," my wife said.

"If I can interview Sophia Loren in dirty overalls, you can go to a clothes party in slacks and a sweater," I replied.

The austerity program was posted in all the rooms in the house and everyone co-operated beautifully from the start. Once they got caught up in the spirit of the thing, I couldn't stop them.

One evening when I came home Joel reported, "The Duponts have two broken windows in their living room and we don't have any."

"Don't cry, son. We'll have two broken windows also." I took his baseball bat and smashed two of the largest panes.

Another time Connie came in tearfully and said, "The La Freres are only eating two meals a day. They have more austerity than we do."

"But he makes more money than I do," I protested.

At clothes parties people started to out-austere each other. One woman, a nouveau pauvre, bragged, "My husband hasn't bought me anything for months."

"If things keep up the way they're going," her husband chimed in, "I'll be in the poorhouse by Tuesday."

Another couple revealed, "We can't afford to go to the Riviera this year."

"We can't afford to go to Versailles," our friends, the Del Ducas, cried.

My wife, who wouldn't be outdone, said, "We've been saving up for four weeks to go to the movies, but I don't think we'll make it."

Many couples had applied for relief, but the ones we

envied the most were the Fauchons, who had managed to get dispossessed and had moved their entire family to a bridge under the Seine.

It's too early yet to know if De Gaulle's austerity plan will work. All we know is that it has changed everyone's way of life.

In some ways it's a pretty frightening thing to see, especially when a good friend comes up to you on the street and says, "Cher ami, would you let me have a couple of unpaid bills until vendredi?"

The Parc With Class

IN THE Academy Award film *Gigi* there is a scene in a park in Paris. The name of the park is the Parc Monceau, and I know it well, since my children are doing time there. There are probably more beautiful parks in Paris—there are certainly larger ones, but I doubt if there is a park in France with as much class.

To give you some idea of what kind of park it is: The kids that play there have hoops, but instead of wriggling in them, they still roll them with a stick. There is no law against hula hoops. It's just that the type of kid who goes to the Parc Monceau is above that sort of thing.

This is not to say that the Parc Monceau doesn't have laws. It probably has more rules than any park of its size in Paris. Dogs, even on leashes, are forbidden to enter the grounds. There is a concrete path running through the center where a child can ride his bike or scooter. But woe to the kid who goes off the concrete on to the footpaths! The grass, of course, is off-limits for children and one risks a prison sentence if he tries to retrieve a ball or wooden airplane.

Since the park is ridden with potential criminals, three gardiens are on duty at all times. Each gardien is armed with a whistle and inside each whistle is a petit pois. Any infraction of the rules brings an immediate blast from the whistle. One blast on the whistle indicates a misdemeanor. Two blasts is a felony. Three blasts can only mean one thing—the child is incorrigible and must be put away for good.

The gardiens could not do their work without the intricate informer system which they have built up.

The children in the Parc Monceau tell on each other.

How the gardiens have built up their informer system is very interesting. When a child commits a minor offense (removing sand from the sand pile without authorization or feeding the swans *stale* bread), the gardien lets him go, on condition that when the gardien needs information on a major crime (theft from the tulip beds, throwing rocks at the fish), the child gives it to him. This informer system has been so successful that 99 per cent of all the crimes committed in the Parc Monceau have been solved.

"Ratting on each other comes easy to children," a gardien explained to me one Sunday morning. "Kids will inform on each other even if they have to make it up."

Clothes play an important role in the Parc Monceau. The majority of the children go to the park with their nannies, and the social standing of the nanny depends on how well dressed the children are. Since the nurses dress the children, and since no nurse would show up with her charge in yesterday's rompers, the parents of the children who play in the Parc Monceau must bear a heavy financial burden. But this makes the park exclusive, more or less like a country club, and the kids who can't afford to change after lunch usually play somewhere else.

One week I rebelled at the laundry bill and said that in the future the children would have to wear the same outfit in the afternoon as they did in the morning. The nurse immediately handed in her resignation.

"The Parc Monceau," she said as she slammed the door, "is not the Tuileries."

You don't see too many lovers in the Parc Monceau. Holding hands is permitted, but smooching is frowned upon. Two people in love might walk through the Parc, but if they want to get serious they're directed to the Bois de Boulogne.

At sunset every night the chains go up on the footpaths and a gardien goes through the park ringing a cowbell, warning everyone the park is to be locked for the night. As it tolls "the knell of parting day—the lowing herd winds slowly o'er the lea"—the nanny homeward plods her weary way—And heaven knows how much it's costing me.

The Jet Age

WE ARE living, so all the ads read, in the jet age. In the next few years jet airliners will be streaking across the sky, making it possible for people to have breakfast in London, breakfast in New York, breakfast in Los Angeles, and breakfast in Tokyo all in the same day. A whole new vista is opening for people who like big breakfasts.

Recently I flew the Pan American Boeing 707 jet from Paris to New York and then back again. It gave me an opportunity to see the jet in action and also gave Pan American a chance to test the cabin under the stress of three very young and violent children.

Both the children and the cabin survived the trip, and as a parent, I can recommend the flight. But I'm not sure the pilot can recommend the children.

There are two classes on a 707 jet—De luxe and Economy. The front of the plane is reserved for De luxe passengers and the back for Economy. De luxe has the following advantages: You go up the same ramp as the pilot and his crew; you have roomy seats; you're plied with liquor and hot hors d'oeuvres, and served a sumptuous meal prepared by Maxim's (there is usually an orchid on your plate), and there is a bar open all night.

Economy has these advantages: You go up the same ramp as the stewardesses; you have seats three abreast; you are not plied with liquor (you can't get or buy a drink in Economy); you are served large sandwiches and coffee, and you have the company of children that stay up all night.

Economy is half the price of De luxe.

Since both classes arrive at the same time, I suggest, in order to save money, wives and children should travel Economy, and husbands should go De luxe.

In my case this was vetoed as soon as it was presented,

and I was forced to travel in Economy class, which is a very sobering experience, even at thirty-seven thousand feet.

As I mentioned before, Economy class has three seats across on each side of the aisle. While this serves the purposes of Pan American very well, it does present problems to the passengers.

It is very rare that three people are traveling together, and most people are either traveling alone, in twos, or in fours. The main problem when traveling with another person is which two out of three seats to take.

My wife was all right, since she had two of the children on her side of the aisle. But I was stuck on the other side with my six-year-old son. He chose to sit next to the window, I sat in the middle, and a stranger was foolish enough to sit in the seat on the aisle.

As soon as everyone had eaten and the stranger had dozed off, my son said, "I have to go."

"Why didn't you go before the lights were turned out?"

"I didn't have to go then," he replied.

My son woke up the man by the simple process of almost breaking his leg.

When we returned after several runs up and down the aisle we woke up the stranger again to get back in the seats.

An hour later my son, after playing with the light, the air conditioning, and the buzzer for the stewardess, declared, "I want a drink of water."

"You don't need a drink of water," I whispered.

"I do too," he cried. Having the choice of either waking up the stranger or everyone else on the plane, we chose the former, and once again pushed our way over his tangled feet.

Later my son said he wanted to tell his mother something.

"Tell her when we get to Paris."

"I want to tell her now."

"Shout it to her."

"It's a secret."

This time when the stranger was awakened he was pretty mad.

"Why don't you sit by the window," I suggested, "and we'll sit on the aisle."

He grunted, mumbled a few words, and moved over next to the window. I stayed in the middle, and my son was placed on the aisle.

Finally the boy went to sleep and so did I. But after a half-hour we were both rudely awakened. The stranger was trying to get past us to the aisle.

"I have to go," he explained apologetically.

It's enough to make a man bring his *own* flask.

The Father's Duty

"ALL right then, why don't *you* take him to get a haircut?"

The speaker was my wife. The statement was made after a long-drawn-out discussion that I made the mistake of starting by simply saying, "The kid needs a haircut."

The kid, it turns out, is six years old and he still can't tell the difference between barbers and doctors. They both wear white smocks and they both have thousands of torture instruments at their disposal. The first time the kid went to a barber he pulled down his pants and waited for the hypodermic needle.

Another time he went to the doctor's office and told the doctor he wanted his hair cut real short.

In either case, he refuses to give them his business. His mother showed me one of these women's magazines whose lead articles, written by "well-known child psychiatrists," are always trying to prove that, with the best of intentions, parents are driving their children into mental homes, manic-depressions, and child marriage.

This particular magazine pointed out that it was the father's duty to take the male child to the barber. Haircuts are tied up with masculinity, and when the mother takes the child to a barber, and the child has a tantrum, he is really revolting against his mother and not the barber, or some jazz like that.

Anyway, there is no point in this modern world in arguing with a child psychiatrist, and I settled the discussion by agreeing to take the boy to the barber.

You would think he would have been overjoyed when he heard the news, but he would have none of it. Then I showed him the article, but he did what I originally wanted to do. He tore the article out of the book and ripped it into shreds.

I had to use strong parental action, "If you go to the barber with me, I'll buy you a toy."

"What kind of toy?" he asked, realizing he was in a strong bargaining position.

"A big toy!" I shouted. "What kind of a slob do you think I am?"

"Will you buy Connie and Jennifer toys also?" he asked, now bargaining for his younger sisters.

"Sure, why not? Then we'll stop by Cartier's and pick up

a diamond bracelet for your mother, and then we'll go over and get a new Citroen for the nurse. There is no telling where we'll stop."

The next morning, bright and early, the two of us took off for the barber. He insisted on going to the same barber I always went to. My barber, for some reason I've never been able to figure out, only takes people on appointment. It's harder to get into his shop than it is to get into Yale, and it's almost as expensive.

When we walked in the barber was surprised to see us.

"You didn't make an appointment," he said.

"It's not for me; it's for my son."

The barber went white. "I don't go into the Algerian section at night, I don't drive over fifty miles an hour in a car, I don't start fights in cafés, and I don't cut children's hair."

I slipped him five hundred francs. "Make an exception. Who will ever know?"

"All the neighbors will know. The doctor who looks at the teeth-marks in my arm will know. The man who sits in this chair after the boy will know. Please take him somewhere else."

I slipped him another five hundred francs. "I've never asked you for anything before. I'll send you customers, I'll print your picture in the paper, I'll wash your car. Please."

"All right, but only this one time."

Before the barber could change his mind I grabbed the boy and stuck him in the chair.

The minute the barber pulled out his scissors the boy let out a scream which brought three bus loads of Gardes Republicaines who thought the paratroopers had landed in Paris.

The boy fought as well as a paratrooper, and the barber couldn't get near his head.

"Perhaps," the barber said, "if you left he would calm down. Come back in a half-hour."

I grabbed a copy of *La Vie Parisienne* and went to a sidewalk café to look at the dirty pictures.

In a half-hour I returned. The barber was just finishing the job. The boy was smiling and seemed to be very happy.

"How did you tame him?"

"I have a way with children," the barber said.

I helped the boy on with his jacket, and then I went to pay the bill. It came to 2,100 francs ($5.00).

"Twenty-one hundred francs?" I shouted. Three more Garde Republicaine trucks pulled up outside. "For just a haircut?"

"For a haircut and a shampoo and eau de Cologne, and a massage, and hair oil."

"Who told you to give him all that?"

"I asked him if he wanted them and he said he did. What could I do?"

I dragged the boy out of the shop and he led me to a toy shop. Then I had to buy him an orange juice. The haircut with the toys and extras cost me exactly $10.50. It's a point the child psychiatrists forgot to mention.

The other point is, at those prices, if there is a choice between the child or the father becoming a manic-depressive over haircuts, I think the head of the family must be spared.

It Pays To Be a Father

ONE of the major differences between America and France is the attitude toward fathers. In America, thanks to comic strips and radio and television programs, the father is treated like the idiot of the family—well meaning, but a stupid clod—who is constantly being saved from calamity by a clever, understanding wife.

But in France the father not only has prestige in the family, he also has the law on his side. There is probably no country in the world that is more concerned with the male parent than France.

A good reason for this is that France wants children. She is even willing to pay for them. The more children a man has in France the more prestige he has in the eyes of the authorities.

For example, the Napoleonic Code formally forbade paternity suits. No unmarried mother had the right to bring the father of her child before justice unless she could prove she was kidnaped nine months before the child was born. This law was established to encourage Frenchmen not to worry too much at a time when France needed soldiers very badly.

In 1912 the code was amended to cover paternity in cases of kidnaping, rape, seduction by fraudulent maneuvers; or a written promise of marriage if the couple were living as man and wife during the critical period, or if the pretended father helped educate the child.

When a woman proves she is going to have a baby she gets the equivalent of sixty dollars, and a bonus of eighty dollars when the baby is born. That's the last time she receives any money if there's a father in the house.

From then on, the father collects a family allocation paid each month by the government.

If the family breaks up and the mother gets custody of the child, she can collect the allocation. But as soon as she gets married again or takes a lover, only the new husband or the lover can draw the allocation.

To prevent the husband or lover from living only on his children, or his mistress's children's allocation, he has to work eighteen days a month.

When a woman is going to have a child the father is given three weekdays off from work. This is not only to help the father recover from the ordeal, but also because there is so much paper work involved with registering the child that the government officials, who should know, figure it will take him three days to complete it.

The best thing in the world is to be the father of three or more children. Besides getting a pension of fifty dollars a month or more, the father also receives a carte de famille nombreuse which entitles him to a 50 per cent reduction in the subway and on buses and trains (75 per cent reduction if you have six children or more) and a 5 to 10 per cent reduction in some department stores.

When a child becomes eighteen, a father of three children loses his reductions, but a father of six or more gets a 30 per cent reduction on transportation for life, because he is considered to be someone who has contributed to the nation's strength and therefore deserves France's gratitude.

Some fathers take their carte de famille nombreuse seriously.

My secretary was sitting on a subway seat reserved for people with priority (invalids, wounded veterans, and pregnant women). A man walked up to her, shoved a carte de famille nombreuse in her face, and demanded the seat. She looked at the card and protested that it didn't give him a priority for a seat. "All the card means," she told him, "is you have a large family."

The man became furious. "How many children do you have?" he asked her.

My secretary jumped up frightened and admitted she had none.

"Well," he said, "I've got five," and he sat down in the seat.

Even the army treats fathers or prospective fathers with respect.

A soldier who becomes a father gets ten days off, and the journey to and from his wife's home is paid. If a man is stationed in the same town where his wife lives (this is for those doing national service), he is entitled to two nights off a week, which means from eight o'clock at night until eight in the morning.

An unmarried soldier has to be in by midnight unless he can prove he is living with a woman, in which case he gets off the same time as married soldiers. To prove that he really lives with a woman the soldier has to get a certified statement from the concierge or the proprietor of the house, or some neighbor who is willing to talk.

The latest statistics say that many more boys are born in France than girls. People say this is because it's so much easier here to be a man than a woman.

Hearken, Teeners, to Nichols and May

THE most important people in America are teen-agers, and as everyone knows they have the most important problems. Hundreds of thousands of movie stars, singers, and disk jockeys are trying to help them, and you can hardly pick up a newspaper or magazine that doesn't have someone giving teen-agers advice.

Mike Nichols and Elaine May, two very successful young American comedians, have been working on an advice-to-teen-agers column for some time and we're happy to be able to print their first one here. In order not to confuse anybody, they're writing under their real names, Atlas Missile and Friday Cohn.

"The trend today," said Atlas, "is to be the moral spokesman of your generation. I'd be very happy to answer any questions about teen-agers and their problems."

"I would too," said Friday.

"Atlas, do you think a girl should kiss a boy on her first date?"

"I don't like girls who play games," he replied.

Friday said, "I feel that if a girl *really* likes a boy, there is no harm in showing it."

"Friday, do you think a thirteen-year-old girl should go steady?"

"I think, if the girl and boy have a real relationship founded on mutual interest, there is no harm in going steady."

"On the other hand," Atlas interrupted, "I think a girl of thirteen shouldn't tie herself up and should play the field until she's ready to settle down at fourteen."

"What's the most important thing a boy admires in a girl?"

Atlas replied, "Good grooming and punctuality."

"And what is the most important thing a girl looks for in a boy?"

Friday said, "Good grooming and consideration."

"What do you think is the cause of juvenile delinquency?"

Friday said, "Insecurity and bad grooming."

Atlas replied, "Bad grooming and lack of religious background."

"What do you think is the cure for juvenile delinquency?"

"Good grooming and security," Friday said.

"And," Atlas added, "proper religious background."

"How far should a girl *go* on a date?"

Friday said, "I think, if a girl has a proper foundation in the home, she will be able to use her own judgment."

Atlas said, "I don't think she should go farther than Connecticut."

"Do you think teen-agers should vote?"

Atlas said, "I think, if they're old enough to support the record business, they're old enough to vote."

"What do you think of teen-age marriages?"

"I think if both parties are mature and from the same planet, a teen-age marriage can work out," Atlas said.

"Should bad skin be a cause for self-consciousness?"

Atlas said, "If you observe habits of personal cleanliness, you don't need to feel bad about having a lot of pimples."

Friday said, "I think, if a girl has a good personality, a boy will forget about her skin."

"Do you think a teen-ager should go to church?"

"I think, if a girl has a good personality, God will forgive her anything," Friday said.

"What constitutes a good personality?"

Atlas said, "Good grooming and punctuality."

Friday added, "Good grooming and being yourself."

"How can you save a teen-age marriage?"

Atlas said, "Stop playing around."

"Should a teen-age girl go with a boy younger than she is?"

Friday said, "I think, if a boy has a good personality, it doesn't matter how old he is. I have a sister who is fourteen and goes with a boy who is seven years old, and they get along fine. I think mutual background is very important."

"How can a boy improve himself?"

"By reading and giving constant attention to good grooming," Atlas said.

"How can a girl improve herself?"

Friday said, "By developing a good personality."

"Who are the people teen-agers should admire the most?"

Atlas said, "President Eisenhower, Albert Schweitzer, and Dick Clark."

"Should teen-agers use lipstick?"

Friday replied, "Only girls."

Fathers Anonymous

I AM in the process now, with the help of several other men, of forming an international organization called Fathers Anonymous. The object of the group is to give up children. Everyone knows you can't kick the habit for good, so the society has not set its sights too high. For a beginning it only hopes to get its members to give them up in the summertime.

As every father knows, a child is the worst thing you can take on vacation. You take one, then you take two, then you take three, and pretty soon you're hooked. There's no escape, and they're with you night and day.

In the city a father can take children or leave them alone. For the better portion of the day he is in a nice, quiet office or factory, and he only sees the children in the evenings. Having been at the office all day, he has a clear mind and can even point out to his wife her faults in the raising of the offspring. The father can fulfill his function as a critic of the household, fair but firm, and can be of great help to the mother, who, being with the children all day, can only see their faults.

But on vacation the father is forced to spend long hours with the children, his senses become dulled, and the effects on the children start to show.

Instead of lying in a beach chair soaking up the sun, he spends most of his time hip-deep in water screaming at the little things to "kick your legs," or thrashing on the sand with somebody else's child over who owns what beach ball.

In the mornings he loses sleep and at mealtimes he loses his appetite. Pretty soon he discovers that his friends, those who have no children, or whose children have grown up, are avoiding him. His wife, who spends most of her time in the hairdresser's, also is avoiding him. He finds himself alone against the world and pretty soon he starts to drink.

It was under these conditions that a small group of us in Deauville decided to form a chapter of Fathers Anonymous.

This is how it works:

The first thing you have to do, as you do with Alcoholics Anonymous is admit to yourself your weakness: you can't take children—not even one child. Once you admit this to yourself, you're on the way to being cured.

You take a pledge that as long as you're on vacation you will let your wife take care of the children.

There are moments, of course, when you will feel like slipping, and at these moments you can call on another member of Fathers Anonymous.

You say in desperation, "I think I'm going to take my kid to the beach." But the member you called rushes over and talks you out of it.

If it's really serious he'll offer to play gin rummy with you or take you to the race track—anything to keep you from going off the wagon.

When he's in trouble he'll call you. "My wife says I've got to take my kid and get his hair cut. I feel like I'm giving in."

"Don't do anything until I get there," you say. Then you

grab your golf clubs and drive over to his house. You explain to his wife that her husband is scheduled to play in a tournament and has to leave right away.

The idea behind Fathers Anonymous is to help yourself by helping the other fathers.

Twice a week FA holds meetings to give the members encouragement. At each meeting the fathers get up and tell what children have done to them.

Each tale is more harrowing than the last one, and it helps the members to know that they are not alone and others have had similar experiences.

The reason for keeping the organization anonymous is that if the wives find out who the members are, they're likely to close FA down.

So far the Deauville chapter is the only one in existence, but, because of the great work they feel they are doing, its members are willing to help chapters get started in other parts of the world.

FA can be summed up in its slogan: "It's no disgrace to have children. It's just a disgrace if you don't do anything about it."

It's Better To Give?

THE giving and receiving of presents, as dramatized by the last pocket-breaking Christmas, usually works a great hardship on the master of the household. I don't know about other people's homes, but it certainly has gotten out of hand in mine. I am not only exchanging gifts with relatives and childhood friends, but with people I don't even know. I have no idea how I ever got myself in this bind, but I am sure it could happen to anyone.

To give you an example of what has happened I cite the following incident:

About seven years ago we met a couple on the boat, whom I'll call Mr. and Mrs. Irving Hoffman. When it came holiday time my wife sent them a Christmas card, which also wished them the best wishes for the New Year.

They in turn sent us a souvenir letter opener from St. Moritz, which, on the surface, seemed to be a friendly gesture.

But when the next Christmas came around, my wife, who keeps the accounts in our house, said, "We have to get the Hoffmans a gift. They sent us a letter opener last year."

I protested that it wasn't necessary and that another Christmas card, perhaps with more elaborate printing, would suffice. But she was adamant. And so she went out and bought a paperweight, which she promptly dispatched with the season's greetings.

The day before Christmas a special delivery package arrived which contained four bottles of Scotch. It was too late to retaliate and my wife's Christmas was spoiled, thinking what the Hoffmans were thinking about us for sending them a lousy paperweight.

The next Christmas I went out and bought them a record album of Beethoven's nine symphonies, which set me back fifty dollars but gave my wife her pride back.

The Hoffmans, who must have had some inkling of what I was up to, sent us a television set. Another Christmas was spoiled.

Fortunately we didn't have to wait for Christmas to get even. We were invited to the wedding of one of the Hoffman daughters and we sent as a gift a silver service from Cartier's.

We were feeling pretty good for a few months, but when my anniversary came around in October I received the complete works of the Encyclopedia Americana in leather bindings.

These people were playing for real.

The next Christmas I bought them a small Van Gogh etching for one thousand dollars and gloated, but not for long. They sent us a set of Louis XIV chairs.

I was all for calling a truce, but my wife insisted I had to go on, even if it meant cutting down on gifts for the children.

"His birthday is in February," she said, "and yours doesn't come up until October. We'll have six months of peace."

I bought him a Vespa scooter for his birthday and delivered it myself just to see him eat his heart out.

It was a blow below the belt, but he recovered fast. Somehow he wheedled out of my wife that my son would be four years old in April.

When April came Hoffman sent ten shares of American Tel and Tel stock as a gift for the boy.

The gift exchanging went back and forth for the next few years without let-up. Feelings were so bitter that we didn't even talk to each other and did all our gift-giving by mail.

This Christmas I decided to fix Hoffman once and for all. I was going to give him a Thunderbird.

But while I was down at the dealer's looking them over, I got a call from my wife.

"Hold off," she cried excitedly. "All we got from the Hoffmans this year was a Christmas card."

"It's just a diversion," I said. "He's going to spring something on us Christmas Eve."

"I don't think so. It was a very cheap card and it had no return address."

"You really think they've given up?" I asked.

"I'm sure of it," my wife said.

"Why, that no good yellowbelly," I chortled. "He lost his nerve. I've got a good mind to send him the Thunderbird anyway."

"Oh, please don't," my wife begged. "He's probably suffering enough as it is, and it is Christmas."

"Okay," I said. "I'll let him off this time, but he better not start up with us again."

The Program for the Next Two Days

(This was written just before my mother-in-law came last spring.)

Paris is always playing host to important visitors. My mother-in-law, Mrs. Marie McGarry, of Warren, Pennsylvania, is arriving in Paris tomorrow for top-drawer conferences with her daughter, Ann. Feverish preparations have been going on for weeks to give her one of the biggest welcomes any American mother-in-law has ever received in Paris. American flags have been hung on every public building, and family authorities have urged everyone to turn out in large numbers to greet her when she arrives in the city.

In order to facilitate matters and make it easy for most people to see her, I'm printing her schedule:

MERCREDI, 1 Septembre

10 heures: Arrival at the Gare de Lyon, where she will be greeted by her grandchildren, her son-in-law, and daughter. She will inspect an honor guard of American Express guards and will be introduced to important baggage porters and ticket collectors.

10 h. 30: She will be placed in a taxi and driven along the quai past the Hôtel de Ville, the Rue de Rivoli, the Place de la Concorde, up the Rue Royale, by the Madeleine and then to the American Embassy, where she will discuss with Embassy officials if any mail has been left for her.

11 h. 55: From the American Embassy, after reviewing the U. S. Marine Guard stationed in front of the building, she will be driven to the Palais Buchwald, off the Parc Monceau, where she will be staying while she is in Paris.

12 h. 50: She will inspect the furniture at the Palais to see if it has been dusted, and then will dispense gifts to the grandchildren.

13 h. 15: She will have a tête-à-tête with her daughter and a light lunch, at which time they will discuss problems of mutual interest.

14 h. 30: She will unpack and send out her dresses to be pressed. She will then go over the dinner menu, making

changes in the rough draft before presenting it to the cook for final approval.

16 h. 10: She will leave the Palais Buchwald in the company of her daughter and Max Wokowsky, a White Russian taxi driver. They will drive down the Champs Elysées to the Avenue Montaigne, and in the presence of Yves St. Laurent and other high officials, she will lay a wreath of francs on the sidewalk in front of Christian Dior.

19 heures: She will drive from Christian Dior's to the bar of the George V Hotel and brief hotel officials on the secret of making a dry Martini.

20 h. 15: She will return to the Palais Buchwald for a large dinner given in her honor by her son-in-law. This will be purely a social event, and no serious business will be discussed.

From 21 h. 30 until three o'clock in the morning she will hold a news conference, giving her daughter all the news about Warren, Pa.

JEUDI, 2 Septembre

8 heures: She will breakfast with her grandchildren and inspect their rooms to see if they are getting enough fresh air.

10 heures: She will drive to the Silvers of Paris Shop on the Square de l'Opera and buy perfume for her family in Warren.

12 h. 30: She will go to the SAS office on the Boulevard des Capucines and reconfirm her reservation back to the United States.

13 h. 15: She will drive out to the Bois de Boulogne with her daughter and get down to her real reason for coming

to Paris—me. She is demanding equal voice in all domestic problems and wants to have a say about future visits of the family to the United States. In exchange, she will give the family the secrets of making an American cheesecake.

Look Out, Mrs. Ford

I SEE by the newspapers and magazines that Mrs. Henry Ford II had a coming-out party for her daughter in Detroit which was supposed to have cost $250,000. I hate to brag but my wife had a party in Paris that cost $250,000 and our daughter didn't even come out once.

According to the reports, Mrs. Ford brought over a French decorator to give the Detroit Country Club an eighteenth-century French motif. Well, my wife went Mrs. Ford one better. She brought over an American decorator to make our eighteenth-century French apartment look like the Detroit Country Club.

It all started because she and her friend, Marjorie Bernheim, decided they had nothing to do on New Year's Eve except possibly go to a night club with their husbands and spend maybe sixty dollars bringing in the new year.

"It's childish to make so much of New Year's," they said to each other, "and a waste of money besides. Let's stay home and play Scrabble, and at twelve o'clock we'll have a glass of white wine together."

We husbands tried to talk them out of it, insisting that they would enjoy going out on New Year's Eve and we didn't care if it cost a few bucks. But they were adamant—

both of them. "You men work too hard for your money to throw it away in night clubs."

So it was settled. But a few days later my wife said to me, "The Kohns are coming over from London and we've invited them to drop by for a drink."

"That's nice," I said. "But can six people play Scrabble?"

"We won't be able to play Scrabble," she said. "They're coming over with the Mores, the Jaffes, and the Shensons."

"Well, maybe we can play charades," I said.

"That would be a lot of fun," my wife agreed.

The next day she said, "Marjorie Bernheim asked Betsy Blair, Lena Horne and Lennie Hayton, and Raoul Levy and his wife to drop by and have a glass with us."

"A glass of what?" I asked.

"Well, we can't have wine. We'll have some champagne. I think we've got a few bottles in the cupboard."

"Can we play charades with that many people?"

"No, but maybe we'll play Twenty Questions."

Nothing happened the next day, but on the following day my wife said, "Did you know the Orshefskys and the Whites were in Paris?"

"What do you mean, did I know it? They live here."

"What I meant was they're in Paris for the holidays so I think we should ask them over."

"It's okay with me."

"But the trouble is that Pres Grover is coming in from Moscow to spend New Year's with them so we'll have to ask him."

"All right."

"But the Kleimans and the Cioffis also promised to spend New Year's Eve with the Whites."

"Well, why don't you ask them?"

"I did."

That evening my wife told me that Marjorie Bernheim had asked Sophia Loren, Carlo Ponti, Jeannette and Paul Emile Seidman, the Markays, the Uffners, her mother-in-law, and the French consul from Geneva.

"It sounds like it's getting to be a party," I said.

"Not really. When Marjorie asked Sophia Loren, I had to ask David Stein and François Reichenbach and Bob Taplinger. Also I spoke to Dorian Leigh this afternoon, and Serge and she aren't going to Switzerland."

"Who is?"

"You know, I think we'd better have some sandwiches in case people get hungry."

"That's a good idea," I said. "Why don't you get some chopped chicken liver from Chez Louis and some rye bread?"

"Well, Marjorie and I thought maybe three turkeys and a ham, baked beans, salad, cheese, and apple strudel would be nice. But your idea about chopped chicken liver is a good one. We'll have that too. But we don't want to bother you with the details. All Alain and you have to get is Scotch."

"Scotch? Do you know Scotch costs seven-fifty a bottle in Paris?"

"Well, we can't just serve champagne. There would be no sense hiring bartenders."

"What bartenders?"

"You've got to have bartenders. I called the caterer this morning and they're sending over three people. Oh, incidentally, we've invited James Jones and his wife,

Maurice Binder, Ray Ventura and his wife, the Snells, and Mr. and Mrs. Kemoularia of the United Nations. He's Mr. Hammarskjold's personal assistant and since he's coming we thought we'd make the party black-tie. Most women like to get dressed up on New Year's Eve."

"We'd better get some more whisky."

"That can wait. You have to move the baby's bed into the other bedroom because we're going to use her room for the fortuneteller on New Year's Eve to tell people what is going to happen in 1960. We found one who's rather expensive but it will be worth while. But I've got good news for you: We hired two people to check the coats. Oh, by the way, *Life* is covering the party, so we'll have to make decorations."

To make a sad story short, we had eighty people and, as I said, it only cost $250,000. It's lucky that Marjorie Bernheim and my wife don't live in Detroit. They would have really given Mrs. Ford a run for her money.

Pay the Two Francs

LIKE I said, we had this party with chopped chicken liver, turkey, ham, and various salads. But since we were giving the party with another couple, the Bernheims, we had to share with them the left-over food and also return a large, silver tray which we borrowed for the party.

So we called a taxi and carried all the food downstairs to go to the Bernheims. Every once in a while you get a taxi driver in Paris who talks to other chauffeurs. In his opinion, every driver on the road is an idiot, and also yellow. To prove it, our driver challenged every car on the Champs Elysées. All of them did prove yellow except one, another taxi driver. They both put on their brakes at the same time, avoiding a smashup, but the tray with the chopped chicken liver, ham, turkey, and salad went flying on to the floor of the taxi.

This was too much for my nerves, and I told the driver to stop the cab and let us off at the Hotel California, on the Rue de Berri. Insulted because we didn't trust his driving, he blamed us for not holding on to the tray when he had to stop to avoid an accident. He said we didn't know how to ride in a taxi. I said he didn't know how to drive one.

At the California I told my wife to get out of the cab. Then I bent down in the cab to pick up the food and the tray.

The driver said, "Pay me now."

I replied, "After I take the food out of the taxi."

He said, "I want my money right now."

I said, "You'll get it after I take the food out of the cab."

"Then we're going to the police," he said. And with the door open he put the cab into gear, and away we went, leaving my wife standing on the sidewalk.

"Nobody refuses to pay me," he said, as he drove madly in search of a police station. Unfortunately he didn't know where one was, and we kept driving around in circles. Finally he arrived not at a police station, but a police barracks where they round up Algerian terrorists.

Four policemen with submachine guns greeted us at the entrance.

It didn't seem like the place for two people who were having an argument about a taxi to get it settled, and it turned out I was right. A police captain came charging out of the barracks, furious that he was bothered. He started bawling out the taxi driver for coming there.

I was enjoying the show when he turned on me and bawled me out for not paying the taxi driver. He demanded my identification papers and told one of the policemen to take me and the driver to a commissariat—a regular police station.

The nearest one was located in the basement of the Grand Palais, where the Paris Automobile Show is held. When we arrived the police lieutenant demanded to know what was wrong.

"Well, we had this chopped chicken liver," I said.

"You had what?" he asked in amazement.

"Chopped chicken liver in the taxi."

Everyone in the station looked up from their work.

"And we had turkey and ham and salad, and he's a lousy driver," I said.

"He won't pay me," the taxi driver said. "He had all the food on the seat, and he didn't hold on to it. Is this my fault?"

The lieutenant scratched his head. "Ça, c'est extraordinaire."

"I wanted to pay him, but I wanted to get the chicken liver out of the taxi first," I said.

"It is not true," the taxi driver said. "His wife knows it's not true."

"Where is his wife?"

"He left her standing in front of the Hotel California," I screamed.

"Calm down," the lieutenant said. "Nothing can happen to her in front of the Hotel California. Where is the chicken liver now?"

"In the bottom of the taxicab where he put it," I said accusingly.

"No," the taxi driver said, "where he let it fall."

Everyone in the police station was breaking up with laughter, and I could see I was losing the battle.

"Do you want to pay him, or not?" the lieutenant asked.

"I'll pay him after I take the food out of the taxi."

"All right," the lieutenant said. "Take the food out of the taxi and pay him."

I went back outside, and while a dozen gendarmes looked on with interest, I put the food back on the silver tray. I heard one say to another "C'est extraordinaire. Foie de volaille haché. C'est plutôt cannibale." ("Chopped chicken liver. It's extraordinary—almost cannibal.")

I paid the taxi driver, refusing to give him a tip, and he drove off, screaming.

I didn't have the nerve to ask the lieutenant to call me another taxi, so I picked up the silver tray and, with the laughter of the police still in my ears, I walked up the Champs Elysées for five blocks.

It will be the last time we give a party with somebody else.

A Letter to the Hon. Santa Claus

THE HONORABLE SANTA CLAUS
REINDEERSVILLE
NORTH POLE

Dear Sir,

I have been informed by certain members of the family that you plan to visit our house on the evening of the twenty-fourth of December. These members, who seem to speak with authority, have assured me it is your intention to leave behind several dozen toys and gifts as well as candy and favors. They say that they have already informed you as to the toys they desire, but naturally they feel if you wish to add anything that they have forgotten, they will put them to good use, and no package left by the chimney will remain unopened.

I was delighted to receive this information, as I was afraid I would have to go out and spend a fortune to buy them all presents. But my son, aged six, and two daughters, aged five and three, insist I don't have to do any shopping as you will take care of everything.

Having just priced several items in a toy shop, this came as a great relief to me.

But they have requested I write to you anyway, as they are afraid that you might have difficulty getting in the house. Our concierge is very suspicious of strangers, particularly those coming down chimneys, and the children fear she may frighten you away as she has done in the past to the egg man, the plumber, and several electricians.

The children suggest, for your safety, that you use the kitchen chimney, which, being in the back of the apartment, cannot be seen by the concierge who lives on the street. The children also suggest you keep your reindeer quiet, as the concierge is a light sleeper.

Joel, my son, knows that you are very busy on Christmas Eve, but he has requested that I ask you, when leaving his gifts behind that they be placed apart from those of his sisters. Last year, if you recall, you left them all in one big heap in front of the Christmas tree and, while he was trying on a sweater his youngest sister opened a package addressed to him, which turned out to be an airplane. I have only Joel's word for this, but he insists his sister broke the airplane before he had a chance to play with it.

This year he was wondering if you would leave ALL his gifts behind the drapes next to the piano. He feels this is safer, and his sisters, caught up in the excitement around the tree, will be unable to find them.

The cleaning woman has also asked me to ask you if this year you would refrain from placing chocolates and chewing gum in the children's stockings. It seems that last year she spent two weeks trying to get chocolate out of the rug and chewing gum off the walls.

As for me, I have a few requests of my own. Would you please not leave any battery-operated toys behind WITHOUT the batteries? It's very difficult to find a store in Paris that sells batteries on Christmas Day, and you are no doubt aware of how worthless toys can be these days without batteries.

Also, if you're going to leave any electric trains this year, would you mind marking on them clearly whether they are for 110 or 220 volts? Last Christmas Eve I spent the better part of the night changing fuses in the house.

A further request (if it isn't any trouble) is, if you're going to drop off any German toys, would you leave the instructions in English as to how to use them? We still have a pair of roller skates from last year that will go only backward.

I might also add that the Assemble-It-Yourself Gas Station, which you left last Christmas with four hundred "Easy-To-Glue-Together" pieces, is still in four hundred pieces. This is nothing against you personally. I know the population is increasing all the time, but I think you should take the engineering abilities of the fathers into consideration before you leave anything that has to be assembled for the sons.

There were several requests in our children's letter that I was wondering if you could ignore. I might mention specifically the automatic hair-trigger machine gun which sounds "just like the one paratroopers use," the electric drum "that plays by just pushing a button," a police siren for a three-wheeler bike, and a teakettle "that whistles when you blow in the spout."

I'm sorry to have taken up so much of your time, but according to the members of my family, you are always open to suggestions.

If you get finished early on Christmas morning, please stop by for a drink. Don't worry about disturbing us—

we'll be up all night trying to put the electric trains together.

Sincerely,
A.B.

Just Give the Operator the Call

A RECENT advertisement in an American magazine caught my eye the other day. The headline said: "HEADING FOR EUROPE? PLAN AHEAD BY PHONE." The copy, underneath a picture of a very contented man, read:

"A good way to smooth your business trip abroad is by calling ahead. You can *talk* to the people you want to see, find out when they're available, decide right there on the phone where and when to meet . . .

"Calling overseas can make *any* trip go smoothly—business or pleasure. And it's easy. Just give the operator your call."

The reason the advertisement caught my eye was that I had received a call from the West Coast on the previous evening, and I had marveled at the way it was all made to sound so simple.

It was midnight, Paris time, when the call came through.

An English-speaking operator with a heavy French accent said, "Monsieur Buchwald, you have a call from America. Can you take it?"

I assured the operator I could.

"Then we will call you back," and she hung up.

A half-hour later the phone rang again. "Monsieur Buchwald, we have a call from America for you. Are you ready to take it?"

I said I was.

"Thank you. We will call you back."

Fifteen minutes later the phone rang again. "Monsieur Buchwald, America is calling you."

"I know," I said.

"Please do not hang up," she warned me.

I promised her I wouldn't. Then I heard the French operator say, "Hello, New York? We have Monsieur Buchwald on the phone."

A voice with a heavy New York accent said, "All right, Paris! I will connect you with Beverly Hills."

There was a pause, and then I heard the New York operator say, "Hello, Beverly Hills?"

The Beverly Hills operator said, "Yes, New York."

The New York operator said, "I have Mr. Buchwald on the phone from Paris."

"Just a minute, New York," the Beverly Hills operator said.

There was a pause, and then I heard her talk to someone on the other end of the line. "We have Mr. Buchwald on the line from Paris."

The person on the end of the line said, "Just a minute. "We're trying to find the party who made the call."

The Beverly Hills operator said, "Hello, New York. We're trying to find the party." The New York operator said, "Hello, Paris, Beverly Hills is trying to find your party." The Paris operator said to me, "Ne quittez pas."

I promised I wouldn't *quitter*.

Then I heard a man's voice. "Hello, Art?"

"Just a minute," the Beverly Hills operator said. "Hello, New York, we have the party on the phone."

"Thank you, Beverly Hills," the New York operator said. "Hello, Paris. Is Mr. Buchwald there?"

The Paris operator said, "Monsieur Buchwald, are you there?"

I said I was.

The Paris operator said, "Monsieur Buchwald is there."

"Thank you, Paris," the New York operator said. "Hello, Beverly Hills. You can go ahead."

"Thank you, New York. You may speak now. How long do you want to talk for?"

"I don't know," the man's voice said.

"All right then," the Beverly Hills operator said. "I'll tell you the charges when you're finished."

"Hello, Art. This is Dave."

"Dave who?"

"Dave . . ."

"I can't hear you."

"Can you hear me now?"

"Yes, I can hear you now."

"Okay! This is Dave . . ."

"I'm sorry, I can't get the last name."

"Operator, operator," I heard him say, "what's the matter with this connection?"

"Just a minute," I heard the Beverly Hills operator say. "Hello, New York, can you hear me?"

"Yes, Beverly Hills. Hello, Paris, can you hear us?"

"Yes, New York, we can hear you."

Then New York said, "They hear you now."

The Beverly Hills operator said, "Go ahead now. Paris can hear you."

"Art . . . Dave . . . want . . . Bardot . . . Can you do it?"

"Do what?"

"I'm going to . . . and I . . . Brigitte . . ."

"I can't hear you."

"Can you hear me now?"

"Perfectly."

"Okay . . . dollars . . . fast . . . Bardot."

"I'm sorry. But I can't hear you. Why don't you send me a letter?"

"Send you a what?"

The Paris operator said, "A letter."

The New York operator said, "A letter."

The Beverly Hills operator said, "A letter."

Dave said, "A letter?"

"That's right," I said. "SEND ME A LETTER."

"Okay," said Dave. "I'll send you a letter."

"Thanks, Dave," I said, "It was swell talking to you."

"I can't hear you."

"I SAID IT WAS SWELL TALKING TO YOU."

"It was swell . . . you. I'll write the . . . on . . . paper."

"You do that, Dave."

"Good-by, Art."

"Good-by, Dave."

The Beverly Hills operator said, "Are you finished talking?"

The New York operator said, "Hello, Paris. Are you finished talking?"

The Paris operator said, "Are you finished talking?"

"Finished?" I said. "How the hell do I know? I don't even know who I was talking to."

2. Tourists on the Brink

The Good American

WHEN Toots Shor, the New York restaurateur who caters to the sporting world, made his first trip to Europe, he had sold his restaurant for over a million dollars, and a new one bearing his name was being built. Since he was between restaurants, so to speak, he decided to come to the Continent. When the news got out that Toots Shor was coming to Europe horrified cries went up from his more sober customers. John Daly, Bob Considine, Earl Wilson, Mickey Mantle, and Yogi Berra tried to talk him out of going.

"I'm a bum who likes booze," Mr. Shor explained, "and those crumbs thought I would get drunk and raise hell over here and make a scene. When they had no success in talking me out of going they contacted J. Edgar Hoover and asked him if there was any law to keep me within the continental limits of Manhattan Island. Hoover looked hard but couldn't find one so he said, 'Let the bum go.'

"So for two weeks before I'm ready to go everyone is calling me up and saying, Toots, be a good American, don't cause no trouble, you're wearing the American flag on your chest, and stuff like that. Everyone says no matter what happens I shouldn't get in a beef with anyone, and I should say Yes to everything. Well, I figure these guys are really concerned about me leaving the country, so I'll take their advice. After all, as long as I can get good booze, I'm not going to cause anybody any trouble."

As Mr. Shor's plane took off for Europe, prayers for peace were held all over the city.

"The plane was supposed to go to Rome," Mr. Shor said, "but instead we got stuck in Shannon. Immediately my wife starts buying out the entire Irish linen production. I tell her that we're going to have a tough time carrying all that stuff around Europe, and it's going to cost us five hundred dollars excess weight. She's of Irish descent, so she replies, 'I've got to help my people.' Well, I start to yell in the airport so she says to me, 'You're behaving like an ugly American.' Immediately I shut up. After all, I promised all those bums in New York.

"Now I'm in Rome and everyone is treating me real good and laying on the wine because they think that since I'm a big American restaurateur I'm an expert. What they don't know is for the whole time I was operating my restaurant in New York I've got three bottles of wine in the cellar, and I could never even sell them. The bums that came to my place drank booze and beer. But every time someone drags out the vino I say Yes, and I'm getting sick to my stomach because I don't dig the grapes.

"We go to Florence, and I'm saying Yes to my wife all the time in public. This costs me like fifteen hundred dollars, but I know the guys back home are going to be proud of me because I'm not making a scene.

"We move on to Venice. It's raining the whole time, but I'm not complaining. The Italians got a right to rain like anybody else, and as a good American, all I can do is wish them Godspeed. From Venice we were to drive to Milan to catch a plane for Paris. The chauffeur asks if we want to stop in Padua for lunch as we have plenty of time. I say Yes. He asks if he can visit his relatives in Padua. I say Yes.

Then he wants to drive by his old school and see how it looks. I say Yes. So we miss the plane in Milan by fifteen minutes.

"I'm ready to let him have it when a vision of Bernard Baruch comes before my eyes. 'Remember, Toots, you are a good-will ambassador.' So I thank the chauffeur for the wonderful drive, and we take a plane out for Zurich, which is supposed to connect with a plane to Paris. But when we get to Zurich there is no room on the plane to Paris, and the man says it was all a mistake and he knows I'll understand. I say Yes.

"The next day we make it to Paris and there are no taxis at the airport except for one and I get it first, but this Frenchman pushes me aside and gets in with his wife. I bring back my fist, but my wife starts whistling 'The Star-Spangled Banner,' and I let the bum get away without a murmur.

"So I finally got to the hotel, and that night I go out to hear the gypsy violinists in Montmartre. They start opening bottles of champagne like there was no tomorrow, and what makes it worse is they're piling up the empty bottles from the other tables under mine. The violinists are all drinking my champagne, and before I leave I get a tab for two hundred dollars.

"I'm ready to wreck the joint when I hear John Daly's voice coming over a loud-speaker. 'Whatever you do, Toots, remember it's their country, and they have their customs. They may seem strange to us, but our customs are strange to them also.' So I pay the bill, and even after I give a tip they're throwing the empty bottles at me as I'm leaving the joint.

"I'm getting into a cab whose meter has been running for

three days, and I can't take it no more, so as the cab is pulling away from the curb I scream at the headwaiters 'You bums!'

"My wife pulls me back in the cab and says, 'As your wife, I can understand such unruly behavior, but as an American citizen, I'm truly shocked.' "

The Ugly American

"THERE ought to be a law against people like that," Anatole Litvak, the American film director, said to me at the Hotel George V.

"Against people like what?" I asked.

"Against people who were on the plane with me yesterday."

"Who were they?"

"They were two Americans, and they got on the plane in Zurich. Everyone was seated by the time they got on and they couldn't get two seats together. The man sat down next to me, and his wife sat four or five rows down on the other side. He had two Air France bags which he put under my seat. He also had two cameras around his neck and about six light meters. He was perspiring and grunting so much I said to him after the plane took off: 'Why don't you take your cameras off?'

" 'You never know, when you're traveling with a group of people like this,' he said confidentially.

"I decided to end the conversation there. Then the steward announced that drinks would be served, but they would have to be paid for. I ordered a beer. The man said to the steward: 'Give me a beer, too.' And then he called out to his wife: 'What do you want, honey?' She yelled back: 'A bottle of water.'

" 'Give the lady a bottle of water,' he ordered the steward.

"The steward brought the beer. 'How much is it?' the man asked.

" 'Seventy francs,' the steward said.

" 'Seventy francs for a beer? I thought drinks were supposed to be cheaper on a plane. How much is that in real money?'

" 'Real money?' the steward asked.

" 'American money,' the man said.

"The steward blanched. 'Fifteen cents.'

" 'Do you take Swiss francs?' the man asked.

" 'Yes, sir, we do.'

"The man took out two Swiss francs (about fifty-five cents). 'What rate will you give me?'

"The steward said: 'The rate is one hundred thirteen French francs to one Swiss franc.'

" 'Is that all?' the man said.

" 'That's all we can give.'

" 'Hey, honey!' the man shouted down the aisle. 'They only give you one hundred thirteen francs for one Swiss franc.'

" 'Well, what do you want me to do about it?' his wife shouted back.

" 'I thought they give you more on the plane.' The man paid for the beer and got back his change.

"I dozed off and then woke up to see the steward standing there with a tray of cigarettes and whisky. 'Would you care to buy any cigarettes or liquor?' the steward asked.

" 'Have you got any Marlboros?' the man asked.

" 'No, sir, we haven't.'

" 'How come?'

" 'I don't know, sir,' the steward said.

" 'Hey, honey, what kind of cigarettes do you want?' the man shouted.

" 'Marlboros,' his wife shouted back.

" 'They don't have any,' the husband said.

" 'What have they got?'

" 'Chesterfields.'

" 'All right, take Chesterfields.'

" 'How much are they?' the man asked the steward.

" 'Two dollars and fifty cents a carton,' the steward replied.

" 'That's a lot,' the man said. 'Hey, honey, how much do we pay for cigarettes back home?'

"His wife yelled back, 'Two dollars and seventy cents a carton!'

" 'Well, they should be a lot cheaper on the plane.'

" 'Please, monsieur,' the steward said, 'there are other people waiting.'

" 'Okay. I'll take a carton. How much is the Scotch?'

" 'One dollar and ninety cents a pint.'

" 'Hey, honey. How much do we pay for Scotch at home?'

" 'Five-ninety a bottle!' his wife yelled back.

" 'How much for a pint?'

" 'We never buy pints.'

" 'Okay,' the man said. 'I'll take it. I only have a twenty-dollar bill.'

"The steward said, 'I can give you the change in francs.'

" 'At what rate?'

" 'Five hundred francs to the dollar.'

" 'Is that all?' "

At this point Mr. Litvak said he became furious and said to the man, "Look, that's a very good rate. I only get four eighty-five to the dollar, believe me."

The man looked at Litvak and said, "How do I know I can trust you?"

"I was so mad I shoved the European edition of the *Herald Tribune* in his face. 'Here's the rate,' I screamed, 'in an American paper!' The man studied the paper and then said, 'If it's an American paper why is it printed in France?' "

Mr. Litvak said: "I was going to hit him right there, right in the jaw, but I just fastened my safety belt and held on to the arms of my seat. Fortunately we landed in another twenty minutes, and I cooled down. As the man got up to leave the plane, he said to me, 'Well, I enjoyed sitting next to you and talking to you. We Americans in Europe have to stick together, or they'll take us all for a ride.' "

Inverted Snobbism

THERE is a great deal of inverted snobbism in regard to tourism. There was a time when people used to brag about the places they visited. Now they brag about the places they haven't visited.

The other night I overheard a conversation among three American couples in a French restaurant.

It went something like this:

"We've been in Paris for two weeks," the first man said, "and we haven't gone to the Tour d'Argent."

The second man replied, "We haven't gone to the Folies Bergère."

The third man said, "Not only have we not gone to the Tour d'Argent and the Folies Bergère, but we haven't even been to the Louvre."

The wife of the first said, "We didn't go to Venice this year. We understand it was so hot and crowded."

The wife of the second said, "We didn't go to Venice either. We also skipped Florence because we have some friends who told us you can buy the same things in Rome."

The third wife said, "We didn't even go to Italy."

The first husband said, "We went to the Brussels Fair, but we didn't go to the Russian exhibit."

The second husband said, "We only went for the day, so we didn't see anything."

The third husband said, "I wouldn't go to the World's Fair if you gave me a million dollars."

"Do you know the Palace Hotel in St. Moritz?" the first wife asked the ladies.

They said they did.

"We haven't been there in years."

"Richard and I flew to Portugal so we wouldn't have to stop in Spain," the second wife said.

"Harold and I were invited to the Spoleto Music Festival

this year," the third wife said, "but we didn't go. We didn't even let them know we weren't coming."

The first husband was studying the wine list. "I can't stand red wine," he said.

The second husband said, "We don't like white wine."

"If it's all the same to you, I hate wine," the third husband said.

The first wife studied the menu and then asked the waiter, "What is the specialty?"

The waiter replied, "Steak au poivre."

She said, "I don't want it."

The second wife said, "We went to Alfredo's in Rome and refused to eat the noodles."

The third wife said, "We went to Maxim's and didn't eat anything."

The first husband said, "We went to Monaco, but we made it a point not to see Princess Grace."

"We were in England," the third husband said, "and we avoided the Queen."

The second husband said, "We were in Rome, but we didn't see the Pope—and we're Catholic."

The first wife said, "We're not coming back to Europe next year."

The second wife said, "We won't be back in the next five years."

The third wife said, "We'll probably never come back."

The first husband said, "If I had to do it all over again I wouldn't have come to Paris."

The second husband said, "You can say that again."

The third husband said, "We're lucky we didn't go to Paris."

"But," protested the first husband's wife, "you're in Paris now."

"What?" the third husband said. He took out his itinerary. "By heaven, you're right. Wait till I get that travel agent when I get home."

The Storyteller

HAVE you ever noticed how helpful wives are when a husband is trying to tell a story? I've noticed it—many times. Just recently I was out with some friends, and one of the wives said, "Dear, tell them what happened to us in Monaco last summer."

"Aw, they don't want to hear about *that*."

"Yes, we do," we all chimed in.

"Go ahead, tell them," the wife said.

"Well, all right," the husband said. "We were driving up from Rome."

"Actually it was Florence," the wife said.

"That's right, Florence," the husband agreed. "We were in Rome before we went to Florence. I was driving."

The wife said, "I don't like to drive on European roads. I think they're very dangerous."

"Yeh, and we came into Monaco."

"Tell them why we drove to Monaco."

"Because there were no rooms in Portofino," the husband said. "But anyway we got into Monaco around five o'clock at night."

"You forgot to tell them what the man at customs said," the wife said.

"It's not important to the story," the husband said.

"I think it's cute," the wife replied.

"If it's cute, tell us," we all begged.

"I don't think it was so cute," the husband said. "He asked if we had any gifts for anyone in France, and we said we didn't know anyone in France, and he said neither did he."

"It was funnier in French," the wife admitted.

"Anyway," the husband said, "the first thing we did was look for a hotel."

"You forget to tell them why we were so anxious to get to a hotel," the wife said.

"We hadn't slept the night before," the husband said. "We thought we'd sleep in Portofino."

"But there wasn't a room to be had in Portofino," the wife said.

"I already told them that," the husband said.

"Well, it's important to the story," the wife said.

"Do you want to tell the story?" the husband asked.

"No," said the wife. "You tell it so much better."

"Okay," the husband said. "So we drove around Monaco for an hour and finally got a room at the Hermitage. We checked into the hotel and went straight to our room. It was summer and still light out, so we pulled the curtains."

"We had agreed," the wife said, "not even to have dinner. All we wanted to do was sleep. Anyway, we've been to Monaco before, and after you've seen the Palace, the gambling casino, and the Onassis yacht, there isn't too much else to see. Wild horses and an invitation from Princess Grace herself wouldn't have gotten us out of that room. That's how tired we were. Go on, dear."

"I set the alarm clock for eight o'clock."

"You forgot to tell them we always carry our own alarm clock," the wife said, "so we don't have to depend on telephone operators to wake us up."

"So I did," the husband said.

"It's important to the story," the wife explained to us.

"Anyway, we went to bed immediately."

"Did you tell them the reason we wanted to get to bed early was because we wanted an early start the next morning so we could drive to St. Tropez?" the wife asked.

"No, I didn't," the husband said. "All right, so we hit the bed and went fast to sleep, both of us."

"Now comes the good part of the story," the wife said. "We were awakened out of the sleep by the alarm ringing, and we got dressed."

"Will you let me finish?" the husband said.

"Of course," the wife said. "It's your story."

"I paid the bill and got in the car and started to drive off. There seemed to be a lot of traffic that early in the morning. And then suddenly, as it got darker and I started . . ."

The wife interrupted. "You see what happened was George had set the alarm for eight, and he had forgotten it was seven when we went to sleep, so actually we only slept an hour, and we were so tired we didn't even realize it. So we paid for a room for an hour, and had to find another place to sleep in Cannes. The extraordinary thing is in France they probably don't think it's strange for people to take a hotel room for an hour. It was very funny, though it didn't seem funny at the time. Anyway, George has been dining out on the story ever since."

The Problems of Traveling With Parents

MOST young people I have met who are traveling with their parents find it very difficult, and there are moments, they have confessed to me, when they wonder why they ever brought their parents in the first place.

Parents never seem to know what is going on. They have preconceived notions of the way children should behave in Europe. And they have no appreciation of what a child has to do to keep his parents from going out of their minds.

In the past year I have talked to many young people about traveling with their parents, and their comments have been very interesting.

Missy Montgomery, the eleven-year-old daughter of Dinah Shore and George Montgomery, told me, "The thing that gets me the maddest about traveling with my parents is that my father won't let me have any wine."

"Why? Do you like wine?" I asked her.

"No, but I like to have it in front of me. Everybody in Europe has a glass of wine in front of them. You don't have to drink it."

Missy Montgomery was traveling with her parents and Mrs. Sidney Korshak, and the latter's two young sons, Harry, fourteen and Stuart, twelve.

Harrry said the thing that got him mad was, no matter what he ordered in a restaurant, everyone stuck their fork into it first.

Stuart said, "What gets me mad is the sight-seeing. Dinah and my mother plan our sight-seeing every morning, and then when it's time to go they say they've got other things to do and we're stuck."

Missy said, "Of course we've got Daddy, but the only reason he comes along is because he doesn't want to go shopping with Mommy."

"I don't mind sight-seeing," Harry said, "if it's just a matter of seeing something. But we're always told we have to see it, and you don't want to see something you're told you *have* to see."

"There is always a constant fight for money," Missy said. "In Paris we used to eat cantaloupe for breakfast until Mommy found out they were two dollars apiece."

"My mother," Stuart said, "is always threatening me with cutting off my allowance because of something I want to do. If you're going to write this for other kids, tell them to get their allowance in advance so it isn't a threat all the time."

"We've only been to three movies since we've been in Europe," Harry said.

"If Daddy wasn't so fed up," Missy said, "we probably wouldn't have seen those."

I asked them what the best way of traveling with parents was.

"The best thing, if you can work it," said Stuart, "is to get your own room. Then they don't know what you're doing. You can stay up all night and they won't know it.

We did that on the ship. If you think they're being too unfair you can always go on a hunger strike."

"We did that in Paris," said Harry. "We had come home from a full day of sight-seeing, and we were in our pajamas, and we were going to eat in the suite when my mother discovered that it said on the menu there was an extra 20 per cent charge for meals served in the rooms. So she insisted we kids get dressed and go down to the dining room to eat. So we went on a hunger strike, and in a half-hour she gave in."

Missy said, "A hunger strike is a good weapon, but shouldn't be used too often."

As far as European food was concerned, the three recommended that the best way to eat in Europe was not to ask what anything was until after you ate it.

Stuart said, "We had octopus one night and didn't know it. It tasted a little like rubber bands. But I think you should try everything once."

Night life is always a problem they told me. Missy said, "I have a girl friend and she's only a year older than me and she got to see the Lido show. But Daddy wouldn't let me go. He said we should be in bed."

"Who's tougher on you, your father or your mother?"

"It's different," Missy said. "Daddy's much more fun to be with in the daytime, but Mommy much more fun at night."

The best part of the trip as far as all three were concerned was the boat. Harry said, "At least on a ship you can have some social life. A kid has no social life when he's on land."

Stuart said, "Also, it's the only place you have any freedom. Parents figure nothing can happen to you on a ship and they leave you alone."

I asked them if they had to do it all over again would they still bring their parents with them.

"I guess so," said Missy. "How else would we get here?"

The Pourboire Institute of Higher Earning

THE Pourboire Institute of Higher Earning, dedicated to the institution of tipping in Europe, had just started its spring session in anticipation of a record tourist season. The institute, which trains people how to win tips and encourage gratuities, invited me to attend the school while it was in session. It was a very revealing experience.

The classrooms were constructed to fit varied situations. The first classroom we entered was built like a bedroom. The students were dressed as waiters, chambermaids, bellhops, and porters. Two of the students, a boy and a girl, were in bed pretending they were clients.

The instructor was shouting at one of the student waiters, "No, no, no. You've done it all wrong. You gave the client a chance to get under the covers. You must enter the room without knocking. When you see the client in her bedroom attire she will be so embarrassed she'll give you a large tip to get rid of you. If she has time to get under the covers, she will not get out of the bed to give you a tip. Now, Jacques, you try it."

The student named Jacques opened the door without knocking and rolled in a breakfast tray. The student pre-

tending to be the woman client screamed, threw a blanket around herself, and shoved a fistful of stage money into Jacques's hands.

"Good, good," the instructor said. "Now let's try a situation with the porters. A man is checking into a hotel room with a woman who is presumably not his wife."

"How do we know she's not his wife?" a student porter asked.

"Because, stupid," the instructor said, "if the woman is unmarried, the first thing she'll inspect is the bed. If she's married, the first thing she'll inspect is the bathroom."

One of the student porters picked up two valises and followed the man and the woman into the room.

"Why are you carrying two bags?" the instructor shouted. "Two bags means *two* porters." Another student rushed to take the other bag. The man and woman clients stood holding hands. The porters put down the bags, bowed, and left.

"Idiots," the instructor said, "you left too soon. Try the lights, see if the drapery cords work, dust the telephone, do anything, but don't leave the room! He'll come through." The student client put his arm around the girl. The porters put the bags on the baggage racks. They looked in the closets, they tried the taps in the bathroom. The student client now had both arms around the girl.

"Don't give up," the instructor said. "Pull open the drawers, count the pages of stationery, fill the inkwells, rearrange the hangers."

Finally the student client thrust his hand in his pocket and pulled out the stage money. He distributed it between the two. The porters left. The student put his arms around the girl again.

"All right," the instructor said. "It's your turn, Marianne."

One of the student chambermaids knocked on the door. The man answered it.

"Do you need any towels?"

"No," the man said, slamming the door.

"Soap. Knock on the door again," the instructor said.

Marianne knocked on the door. "Monsieur, here is a cake of soap."

"Thank you." He slammed the door again.

"Hangers. Don't forget the hangers"—the instructor was jumping up and down.

Marianne knocked on the door again. She held out some hangers. This time the client gave her some stage money and said, "We don't want to be disturbed."

"Very good, Marianne. Now let's do the check-out. Everybody on their feet. The couple is checking out. You're all in this. Hurry up now. That's it. Line up by height outside their door."

Thirty students lined up by the door. The couple started to leave the room. One of the bellhops stopped him. "You forgot your shoes, monsieur." The student client took the shoes and gave him a tip. The chambermaid bowed. "Bon voyage, monsieur." The porter brushed off the lady's coat, and so on. They bowed in such a way that the couple couldn't pass without giving them a tip. When he reached the end of the line the student client ran out of stage money.

"Don't relax," the instructor yelled. "Everyone down into the lobby and line up again. Run down the stairs. The elevator boy will slow the client down. Hurry, hurry."

The thirty students ran down the stairs to another classroom which was built like a hotel lobby and lined up once again. Some of them had changed jackets so the clients wouldn't recognize them.

"Au revoir, monsieur." "Goodbye, sir." "Come back soon."

The student client had replenished his supply of stage money and was passing it out again. The line extended out into the street. As each student was tipped, he rushed from the beginning of the line to the end. The couple finally managed to get into a taxi.

"How much money did you get away with?" the instructor asked the student client, in the discussion period.

"I still had two hundred francs left."

The instructor glared at the students and said, "Well, you can't win them all."

Fulfilling Requests

THE trouble with going to Europe is everyone is always asking you to do something for them. They either want you to shop for them, look up somebody, pick up something, or drop off something, or, at the least, keep busy while you're away.

"When you're going to Europe," Bill Dana, a writer friend, told me, "your friends experience a combination feeling of envy and happiness. They're envious that you're going, but happy that you can bring something back for them.

"For months previous to your departure you are accepting lists of errands and chores that they ask you to do, and because you have a certain sense of guilt about going, you accept the lists without much of a protest.

" 'After all,' you rationalize, 'if they were going they would do the same for me.' "

Mr. Dana took a list out of his pocket. "This," he explained to me, "is just my pocket-book edition. The larger list is in my room on the trunk rack.

"Look at this."

He showed me a request. "Buy two copies *Lady Chatterley's Lover*, three Henry Miller paperback editions, and see if you can find any French editions of *Fanny Hill.* Don't declare at customs."

" '*Lady Chatterley's Lover* is on sale in the States now," I told him.

"I know," said Mr. Dana, "but this guy wants the expurgated version."

He showed me another request. "Please look up Mlle. Françoise and tell her I'm sorry. She'll know what I mean."

"The result of delivering this message," Mr. Dana said, "is that I almost wound up being named a corespondent in a divorce trial in Oberammergau.

"Here's another one," he said, going through the book. " 'Go to Pompeii. There is a guide there who will look other way for two hundred lire. Pick me up pink marble head to go in dining room.' This is from my sister-in-law. So I go to Pompeii and I give the guy two hundred lire for looking the other way. Unfortunately another guide who is looking the other way for some other tourist sees me trying to swipe the piece and arrests me. It cost me fifty dollars to get out of that one.

"The worst, of course," Mr. Dana said, "are the shopping requests. Here's one. 'Please go to shop off S. Marco Square in Venice. There is a souvenir shop specializing in Italian things. Ask the man—he speaks a little English—if he has any more compacts like the one he sold the woman in the white hat last summer in August. I'm sure he'll remember me because I had my camera with me. I forget the name of the shop, but it was just off the square and it had Venetian glass in the window. If he has any more get me three, but don't pay more than five dollars for them.' This is from my aunt.

"Here's one from Kay Thompson. 'Go to shop next to George V and ask them what happened to sweaters I ordered six months ago which they promised to send.'

"I went there and saw the manager of the store, who said they weren't ready yet. He was surprised. 'I didn't know it was a rush order.'

"Here's a beauty," said Mr. Dana, tearing out a page. "From one of the guys in the office: 'Get me Mark 62.9ZL view finder for Contactaxta camera model OL1356. Reflex 35-millimeter telephoto wide-angle tripod. Do not get Mark 62.8ZM for Contactaxta model OL1356 reflex millimeter as it doesn't fit. At the same time make sure the Mark 62.9ZL view finder is not for the OL1355 model, which won't fit on the OL1356. You can pick them up anywhere in Germany.'

"He was right. I could pick it up anywhere in Germany—but what he forgot to say was *East* Germany. I finally made a trip to East Berlin to get it. When I got back to West Berlin there was a telegram waiting for me. Forget request for Mark 62.9ZL view finder. Macy's just had a sale on them.'

"Am I boring you?"

"No, not at all," I said.

"All right," Mr. Dana said, "here's one last one I want to show you. 'Please pick up a painting for us in Paris to fit our living room. It should be two feet by three feet, and anything you like we're sure we'll like. But for heaven's sakes no abstracts, because it doesn't go with the rest of the room. Also we're not too keen on still lifes, and Robert hates landscapes. I'm not fond of portraits and flowers are pretty dull. To give you some idea of the kind of thing we want, the curtains are green and the sofa is a burgundy red. The rug is beige. Please don't spend more than thirty-five dollars. I'm sure you can find a young French boy who will be another Van Gogh. Don't ship it home as we'll have to pay duty on it. Use your own discretion, but for heaven's sakes no fruit and no nudes. Outside of that we'll leave the subject matter up to you. Lay out the money and we'll pay you back—if we like it, hah, hah, hah.'

"Sometimes," said Mr. Dana, "you wonder if a trip to Europe is worth it."

Little-Known Festivals in Europe

THERE are many folk festivals in Europe, some dating back to time immemorial. There are also music festivals, film festivals, drama festivals, dance festivals, bullfight festivals, and gastronomic festivals.

While the major ones are publicized, there are others

that rarely receive the attention they deserve. It is a pity that more people don't know about them.

For example, there is the Gazpacho Festival, which is considered one of the most unique and colorful festivals on the Continent. Every year on the second Tuesday after Mother's Day the people of Gazpacho get dressed up in their colorful Tequilas, Rizzotos, and Hakims, and at dawn they start to dance through the streets of the town, stopping occasionally at the café to refresh themselves with ice-cold glasses of the strong Motherherring wine.

The procession takes a circuitous route through the narrow streets of Gazpacho, where more celebrators join in the parade while others wave gaily from decorated windows. Finally, at around ten o'clock in the morning, the procession, led by the town band, arrives in the Gazpacho Main Square, where tourists who have paid anywhere from six thousand to ten thousand fandangos are seated in specially built stands to watch the hilarity.

In the exact center of the square is a pile of cobblestones which the natives have collected all year long. The natives dance around the pile and then, at a signal from the mayor, each person picks up a cobblestone and suddenly starts throwing it at the tourists. No tourist can escape, and when all the visitors are stoned to death the festival is considered over. After the square is cleaned up the natives take off their colorful costumes and put them away for another year.

There have been some protests from neighboring towns about this fiesta, but the people of Gazpacho always reply, "We don't like tourists and this usually teaches them a lesson."

The Feuerfest in Gesundheit is also one of the most

colorful in Europe. The story goes that in 1190, on the day before the crops were to be brought in, Black Frederick, the Prince of Lower Gesundheit, ordered all the crops of Upper Gesundheit to be burned so Lower Gesundheit could raise its price.

Good King Achoo of Upper Gesundheit became so enraged he ordered his people to set fire to all the crops of Lower Gesundheit, and for the next few years no citizen of either Lower or Upper Gesundheit would leave his house without a flaming torch.

From this humble beginning was started a custom which has come down from generation to generation. Every year since 1190, on the day before the harvest, the natives get dressed up in their colorful costumes and set fire to each other's lands.

In the evening there are fireworks, and street dancing, lighted by the fires which can be seen for miles around.

The bitterness has long since died between Upper and Lower Gesundheit, but neither side will break with tradition.

And although the natives lost all their crops and haven't eaten well since, Feuerfest is, for them, the high spot of the year.

The last exciting event worth mentioning, though there are hundreds more if we had the room, is the Children's Fair at Kecknivek. Every year the parents of Kecknivek dress up their children in their native costumes and bring them to the colorful fairgrounds, where they are sold.

Prices range anywhere from seventy zaphnicks for a little girl to three hundred zaphnicks for a strapping boy.

Beside finding the festival a major source of its income,

Kecknivek prides itself on the fact it has never had a juvenile delinquency problem. The town is considered a model community throughout the rest of Europe.

In the evening there is street dancing and fireworks, and everyone has a good time.

The Children's Fair always takes place the first week in June so it will save the parents the expense of sending their children to camp.

The Miracle Drugs Abroad

SOME time ago the American boss of a friend of mine told the friend, "I admire you people who live abroad. You don't take pills. In America we're always taking a pill for something or other. We're becoming a nation of hypochondriacs. But you people here don't depend on pills."

My friend agreed. "We can't get any."

Well, it was a good story, but not necessarily true. The majority of Americans coming to Europe are weighted down with every imaginable medication prescribed by family doctors. Each one is a miracle drug in its own right, and I haven't met an American tourist yet who isn't willing to share his medicines with the less fortunate people who live abroad.

Just recently I had the occasion to see how many Americans will come to the aid of their fellow men. It all started off when I complained at a dinner party of having a sore throat.

"I have just the thing for you," the hostess said. "It's Slipawhizdrene. You take one every two hours."

One of the guests said, "Slipawhizdrene is outdated. My doctor gave me Heventizeall. It doesn't make you as sleepy, and you only have to take two every four hours."

"I left the United States two weeks after you did," another woman said, "and Heventizeall has been superseded by Deviltizeall. I have a bottle at the hotel, and if you stop by I'll give you some."

The only Frenchman at the table said, "Why don't you gargle with aspirin?"

The people at the dinner couldn't have been more shocked if he had said a four-letter word. The Frenchman's American wife was so embarrassed she almost broke into tears.

He looked around helplessly. "But what did I say wrong?"

The husband of the hostess tried to smooth things over. "You see, René, in America we have gone beyond aspirin. You French believe in food; we believe in miracle drugs."

"They're all barbarians," muttered one of the Americans.

After the dinner I stopped by the hotel and picked up an envelope of Deviltizeall. I took two before I went to bed. At four in the morning I no longer had my sore throat, but I was violently sick to my stomach. I remained in this state until morning. I had a luncheon date with a Hollywood producer, but I couldn't eat anything.

"I've got just the thing for an upset stomach. It's called Egazzakine. Here, take one now, and one at four o'clock."

I took the proffered pill, and in a half-hour my stomach settled. Only now, my eyes started to run, and I began sneezing.

Making my way blindly to the office, I ran into another American friend in front of the Lancaster Hotel. He recognized the symptoms immediately. "You've probably got an allergy. Come upstairs and I'll give you something for it."

We went up to his room, and he took out a leather case filled with various bottles.

"Let's see," he said, reading from a slip of paper. "The yellow-and-black ones are for jaundice, the green-and-blue ones are for pneumonia, the white-and-red ones are for rheumatism, the pink-and-beige ones are for heart trouble—oh, yes, the brown-and-purple are for allergies. Here, take two now, and two at four o'clock."

"But," I protested. "I've got to take the Egazzakine at four o'clock."

"Don't do it," he warned. "That's what you're probably allergic to."

I took the brown-and-purple capsules and went to the office. In about an hour, my tear ducts had dried up and I had stopped sneezing.

I felt perfectly well, except I couldn't move my left arm.

I reported this to my friend at the Lancaster, who said, "The doctor warned me it happens sometimes. He gave me something else in case it did. I'll send it over with the bellboy."

The bellboy brought over some orange-and-cerise tablets.

I took two, and it wasn't long before I could lift my arm again.

That evening during dinner I discovered I had my sore throat back. But I didn't mention it to a soul.

A Tourist Diary Form

IT IS very hard for people who travel to keep diaries. By the end of the day most tourists are too tired to write down what they have done. So as a public service I am printing a handy, tourist diary form. All the tourist has to do is fill in the blank spots and he will have a perfect record of the day. Unfortunately I can print only one per book, so if you want any more rush down to your local bookstore right away.

Dear Diary,

Today we are in .... The weather was .... but we still managed to get in some sightseeing. We went to the .... Cathedral, the .... Church, the .... museum, the .... tombs, the fountains of ...., the .... monument, the ruins of ...., the American Express, and a little restaurant I forgot the name of. I got some terrific still pictures in color, but my movie camera jammed on me and I'm not sure I got much footage.

The guide told us Americans were .... in the country. He assured us if war came the .... would fight. He told us a .... makes .... dollars a month, which is one-quarter of what a........ ...... would make in the United States. It's very interesting to talk to the natives of the country and get firsthand information on what's going on.

In the afternoon my wife went shopping and she must have bought the whole town up. She said she had to buy gifts for ...., ..., ..., ..., ..., ..., ..., ..., ..., ..., ..., ..., ..., ..., ..., ..., ..., ..., ..., and ....

I told her it was ridiculous for her to buy so many gifts, so she cut our .... and ...., whom we don't like anyway.

It's a small world, because we were in this .... shop, when whom should we bump into but the ....s, who have a house next to us at .... Beach. We didn't even know they were in Europe. It was good to see someone from home and to talk to someone who spoke .... They said they had just come from ...., and that's where we're going next. They said we could forget about ...., because they're just out to get the tourists. .... gave my wife the names of some shops in ...., where we're going after we leave .... We decided to have dinner together at the .... My wife insisted we invite them, but I was under the impression they invited us. It didn't make any difference, because when the check came .... paid for it.

While we were in the restaurant we met some people from .... who knew the ....s from .... I had gone to school with .... and we invited them to join us. They were going to ...., where we had just come from, and we gave them the names of some good restaurants and shops. But we warned them about ...., which is just a tourist trap.

After dinner we went to the .... cabaret. Everyone had champagne, which cost .... dollars a bottle. They're sure out to take the tourists here. They had some acts, but I've seen better on the .... television show.

We went to another club after that, called the .... My wife said it was my idea, but it was ....'s, and I had to go along or be a bad sport.

We didn't get home until four in the morning, and then my wife spent the next two hours telling me why she didn't like the ....s. She had made a date to go shopping with her next day, and she said she was going to cancel it.

I said why did she make a date with .... in the first place if she didn't have any intention of keeping it. She said I was probably on her side and " ....., ..., ..., ..., ..., ..., ..., ..., ..."

I said I was sorry I brought it up, and she said she just wanted to say one more thing and then she'd be quiet.

She said: "..........., ..., ...; ...., ..., ..., ..., ...? ...., ..., ..., ..., ..., ..., ...

........, ...; ....? ....
....
.... Good night."

Just as I was dozing off, she said, "....................
.... And don't forget to leave a call for eight o'clock."

He Was Looking for a Foreign Car

My good friend Alan King, the comedian, was in London pricing cars.

"Most wives," he said to me, "when their husbands are going to Europe, ask them to bring home a bottle of perfume. Not my wife. She said, 'If you're going to Europe would you mind bringing me home a foreign car?' "

"I said, 'What do we need a foreign car for? We've got two cars now.' And she replied, 'Because everyone in the neighborhood has a foreign car. How does it look for me to drive up to the supermarket in a Cadillac? The people will think you're out of work. Besides, were the only ones left with a large car, and I'm sick and tired of driving all the neighbors' kids everywhere because their parents have no room for them.'

"This last argument made sense. As a matter of fact, I myself had felt the strain between ourselves and the neighbors. My kids took the brunt of it at school. The other kids in school became very cruel and used to shout at my kids, "Your father has an automatic shift,' and 'Your mother has an engine in the front' and stuff like that.

"My kids used to come home in tears. 'Eric Gordon's

father gets sixty miles to the gallon,' they would say. Or 'David Jaffe's mother has the smallest wheelbase in the neighborhood.' These are harsh words for a kid to throw at his father, so I promised the family I wouldn't come back unless I brought a foreign car.

"It actually wasn't a bad deal. If I brought back a foreign car, I'd be a hero, and if I decided not to come back, what could I possibly lose?

"So when I got to London I started looking for a foreign car. It wasn't as easy as you might think. I asked the concierge at the hotel where I could buy a foreign car, and he sent me hell-and-gone to the other side of London. There was a showroom with a large sign "Foreign Cars," and I went inside. You know what they were selling? Buicks, DeSotos, Fords, Chevys, and Studebakers.

"I said to the guy, 'I want a foreign car,' and he said, 'These *are* foreign cars. They've just been imported.'

" 'NO, you don't understand,' I said, 'I want to see a Jag or an Aston Martin or an MG or something like that.'

" 'Oh,' he said with disdain. 'You want a *domestic* car. We don't handle them. Our clientele prefers something more interesting. As a matter of fact, I had a father come in the other day who bought one of my American cars. He said all the children in the neighborhood were making fun of his child because he owned a Bentley.'

"Well, anyhow, I got out of there in a hurry and started shopping on my own. I went back into town and passed a Rolls Royce dealer. Naturally I wasn't in the market for a Rolls Royce, but all the advertisements say the noisiest thing in a Rolls Royce is the clock, and I wanted to know what time it was.

"The salesman who greeted me was wearing striped pants and a tail coat. I felt pretty uncomfortable in my brown pin-striped Brioni suit.

" 'Playing golf?' he asked, to put me at ease.

" 'No,' I replied. 'Just puttering around the garden.'

"He didn't laugh, so I said, 'I'm interested in a Rolls Royce.'

" 'But is a Rolls Royce interested in you?'

" 'I don't know,' I said. 'Why do you ask?'

" 'If you'll permit me, sir, we like to know a little about our prospective customers. Where are you from?'

" 'New York,' I said.

"He didn't seem too crazy about this, so I said, 'But I live in the country—Forest Hills.'

"That helped a little. Then he said, 'Has anyone in your family ever owned a Rolls Royce before?'

" 'Sure,' I said. 'My father always drove one to pick up his relief checks during the Depression. My uncle has one in Odessa now which he is using for harvesting wheat. What is all this stuff?'

" 'Please, sir,' he said, 'we wouldn't want out car to get in the wrong hands. Now what do you intend to do with the motorcar if you buy one?'

" 'Throw parties in it, open up a night club, maybe a gambling casino. Look, all I want to do is ride in one.'

" 'We'll do the home study later,' he said. 'For the moment, which model are you interested in?'

" 'Why? Are there different ones?'

" 'Well, there are the standard models and custom-built ones.'

" 'What's the difference?'

"He looked at me as if I were mad. 'The difference between buying a suit off the rack and having one made for you.'

" 'I don't care, just give me one off the floor.'

" 'Oh, we can't do that,' the man said. 'All these cars on the floor are used models.'

" 'They look pretty new to me.'

" 'But,' he said, 'Eyes have looked on them. We wouldn't think of selling you a car that someone else has *seen.*'

"To make a long story short, I got one of the custom-built models with a bar in the back and a seat that turns into a bed and a luggage compartment with luggage to match the seats.

"Besides a chauffeur I need a footman to take out the luggage, a bartender to mix drinks, and a chambermaid to change the sheets when somebody takes a nap.

"But my wife is going to be very happy. We'll be the only people in the neighborhood who own a twenty-thousand-dollar house and a thirty-thousand-dollar car."

The National Italian Sport

THE site for this year's summer Olympics is Rome. The Italians are great sports lovers, and the national sport of Italy is Far Rumore (translation—"to make noise"). The sport originated some time in the Middle Ages in Sicily when it was discovered that visitors to the island were sleeping instead of buying souvenirs in the shops.

This infuriated the Sicilian merchants so much that they hired men and women to stand under the windows of tourists and shout at each other.

Later on they hired pig beaters and donkey-cart owners to drive around the main streets at three and four in the morning. The screaming of the pigs and the rattling of the carts drove the visitors out into the streets, where they had nothing else to do but shop. The Sicilian merchants prospered, and the idea soon caught on on the mainland.

Today there isn't a town in Italy that doesn't have several first-class Far Rumore teams. While refinements have been added, the objective of the sport is still the same—to keep tourists from sleeping.

In some cities, motor scooters and Ferraris have replaced the pigs and donkey carts, and the automobile horn is as important to the Far Rumore player as the cape is to the matador.

Roger Price, who was recently in Naples, reports he was there for the regional tryouts, which were held in front of his window at the Hotel Excelsior. The people around Naples, he said, shun modern methods and prefer to holler.

"The champion hollerer of Naples had died since the previous tryouts," Mr. Price told me, "and so they held a minute of noise for him.

"Then they got on with the games. The tryouts are always held between midnight and eight in the morning. There are different categories. But the results are always the same. The one who wakes up the most tourists, wins.

"There are the singles matches, when each participant must holler alone. Then there are the mixed doubles, when husbands and wives compete against each other. Finally there are the team matches, in which teams composed of men who have consumed a bottle of wine apiece start shouting at each other.

"The teams are cheered on by spectators, and there is always a great deal of arguing after the matches about who made the most noise, the teams or the spectators."

In Rome the mixed doubles are held between teams of sports cars and motor scooters on the Via Veneto. The mufflers are taken off the vehicles exactly at midnight, and the contest goes on until dawn. It isn't necessary for the vehicle to move; as long as their motors are running they are in the game.

As you go farther north, Far Rumore takes on a different flavor. In Florence William Dana, an American tourist, reports, Far Rumore is played with garbage pails, and the teams are made up of the building superintendents on one hand and the garbage collectors on the other. For years, the building superintendents won the contest, but recently the garbage collectors have been winning, thanks to a new coach named Giuseppe Casaldiavolo. The coach invented the famed "Casaldiavolo pass," in which the garbage pail is slammed against the side of the truck before the garbage is emptied. Since then the tourists have given the nod to the collectors, and the superintendents are looking around for a new coach.

In Venice Far Rumore is played between the gondoliers and the motorboats. The gondoliers used to sing to keep tourists awake, but in recent times, every time they started, the motorboat owners revved up their engines and drowned them out.

This so infuriated the gondoliers that they brought in a team of hollerers from Naples, and now, instead of singing, the gondoliers holler oaths at the motorboats. Since then the matches have been even.

Even in the smaller towns Far Rumore is played. Mr. Price reports he was in a small town near Genoa, where, instead of hollering or racing their motors, the peasants played by banging a stick against his car.

The world record for a tourist sleeping in Italy is three hours and forty-seven minutes. It's held by a ninety-year-old Frenchman named Alain Bernheim, who lost his hearing aid an hour before he went to sleep, and the motor scooter assigned to his window ran out of gas.

A Genuine Fraud Is Caught

Not so long ago I wrote a story about a fellow named Smith. His name wasn't Smith, but at the time our lawyers wouldn't let us use his "real" name which it wasn't.

Smith said he was Dudley Nichols and he was the famous screenwriter. The real Dudley Nichols, one of the great Hollywood screenwriters, died quite recently.

The phony Mr. Nichols was trading in on the real one's reputation in Rome. He promoted the late Mario Lanza for more than ten thousand dollars, promising he was going to write a screenplay for him. He promoted other people into giving him money to start up Little Leagues for baseball in Italy. He said he was a member of Alcoholics Anonymous and also a patron of Strategic Air Command. When we met in Rome he was entertaining a crew from SAC who had come up from Tripoli on leave.

After his fling in Rome "Mr. Nichols" came to Paris and called me. By this time I knew he was a phony, but my wife didn't, and she invited him to a cocktail party. He brought her a hundred-dollar bottle of perfume. I finally asked him to leave when he started promoting several of the guests. My wife was upset at my rudeness because she pointed out that even though he was an impostor, he did bring her a hundred-dollar bottle of perfume. I insisted we should have given the perfume back, but she said that would have hurt his feelings more than anything. A few days later we received a call from a perfume shop. "Mr. Nichols'" check had bounced higher than the Eiffel Tower.

A few weeks later, "Mr. Nichols" showed up in Germany and left hot checks all over the place, including one for one thousand two hundred dollars for air transportation. He was being sought at the time by the Italian police, the French police, the German police, Interpol, the FBI, and Air Force Intelligence.

Finally everyone in Europe could relax, because "Mr. Nichols," whose real name is Glenn Davis Castle, was arrested in Fort Worth, Texas, for stealing $125,000 worth of American Express money orders from a printing plant of the International Business Machines Company.

Castle had probably one of the greatest flings of any ex-convict who has visited Europe in the past few years. His past record was an amazing one for a man who was only forty-one years old. He was arrested thirty times for alleged larceny, forgery, and parole violation. He jumped bail in Chicago before coming to Europe.

When Castle was caught in Fort Worth he spoke the truth for the first time in fifteen months. He said, "I'm just a genuine fraud. . . . It takes a lot of work to be a genuine fraud."

Castle apparently managed to fool everyone because he was impersonating someone that many people had heard of but never met. He also had a passport made out to a Dudley Nichols which he used for identification.

But his best gimmick was when he announced in Rome that he was going to help Italian kids learn how to play baseball. Who could doubt the intentions of a man who was strongly in favor of baseball? Besides, he had excellent credentials. He carried around a baseball with the forged signature of President Dwight Eisenhower.

This was enough to make many public-spirited visiting Americans give him money. One of the few who turned Castle down was Paul Getty, the billionaire.

A third factor in Castle's favor was his posing as a member of Alcoholics Anonymous. He created sympathy among strangers.

When we saw Castle at Mario Lanza's home he said he was trying to help Mr. Lanza give up drinking. He himself had known the evils of drink and he was dedicated to saving others. The next time we saw Castle he was stewed to the gills.

Castle also knew that one of the best ways of working as a genuine fraud was to pick up bar and dinner checks. Americans tend to believe that a man who grabs the check is a good guy and a man who lets you grab the check is a bad guy.

And as far as some American wives are concerned, any man that brings them a hundred-dollar bottle of perfume has to be legitimate. Otherwise, what is there left to believe in?

3. *Soup and Some Nuts*

"Yes, Sir, That's My Baby"

THERE are very few top playboys in circulation these days. Rubi Rubirosa is married. Aly Khan is a United Nations delegate, and his son, the young Aga Khan, has yet to do justice to his father's footsteps.

This leaves the field pretty much to Francisco "Baby" Pignatari, a wealthy Brazilian industrialist who is probably one of the hardest-playing bachelors in Europe.

I was very fortunate to have lunch with Mr. Pignatari and his social secretary, Mr. Richard Gully, at the Ritz. Having latent playboy tendencies myself, I was interested in knowing how Mr. Pignatari operates, in hopes of picking up some pointers.

At first Mr. Pignatari was reluctant to discuss his operations, not out of false pride, but because he was afraid if he gave away too many secrets, his activities in the future might be slowed down. But I pointed out, and he agreed, that publicity might help his activities rather than hinder them.

Mr. Pignatari said that to be a successful playboy one must have the confidence of the barmen and the headwaiters of all the leading hotels and restaurants.

"They're the ones," he said, "who are able to give you the pertinent details on an attractive woman, the ones that are so necessary before one makes an approach."

"One of Baby's best approaches," Mr. Gully said, "is to

send a surprising gift to an attractive woman. If, for example, someone is selling flowers in a restaurant, Baby may buy the whole tray and tell the waiter, 'Send these flowers over to that lady with my compliments as a tribute to her beauty.' Or he may send out for a large bottle of perfume. He is never fresh."

"Would you write a nice note with a gift?" I asked.

"Baby never puts anything in writing," Mr. Gully said. "He's the only person I know who gives a girl a diamond bracelet without a card."

"Do you know what flatters a woman more than anything else?" Mr. Pignatari asked me.

I said I didn't.

"It's a long-distance telephone call."

"It's one of Baby's greatest techniques," Mr. Gully said. "He calls women all over the world and they're delighted. It's a wonderful way of building for the future. Baby has lady friends in every town."

"It also saves you writing letters," Mr. Pignatari said.

"One of the things that helps a playboy," Mr. Pignatari told me, "is being written up in the newspapers."

"Baby," said Mr. Gully, "has a pre-sold audience. He has all the requisites for being a glamour boy. There are so few who have ALL the requisites."

"What are they?" I asked, hopefully.

"Baby has sex appeal, charm, and money, and he's a good host. He entertains fabulously. He always has two cars with him, and when he meets an attractive girl he lets her use one of them, with a chauffeur, of course. He speaks four languages, and he's been married two times."

"How would being married two times help someone like Mr. Pignatari?"

"If a playboy hasn't been married," Mr. Gully replied, "the women feel there isn't a chance for them. This way there is always hope."

"I am not an adventurer," Mr. Pignatari said. "I always give things to women and I never exploit a friendship. I am an industrialist, and I built up the business all myself."

"Baby is one of the most successful men in South America," Mr. Gully said. "He talks to Brazil almost every day on the phone."

Mr. Gully said the fact that Mr. Pignatari is a successful businessman appeals to women. "This is a new age. The former glamour boys were dukes and princes and marquises. Now, women prefer attractive self-made men."

Mr. Pignatari revealed he doesn't waste much time romancing a girl. "I have instincts which tell me right away if it's worth my while. The first time we look at each other I know."

"What do you know?" I probed gently.

"I just know."

"Another thing that attracts women to Baby," said Mr. Gully, "is that he likes to do dangerous things. He drives fast, he flies his own airplane, he skis, and he can swing from a trapeze. Most men have a tendency to play it safe, but women like a man who lives dangerously."

"What else?" I inquired, losing all hope I could ever be a playboy.

"A very glamorous woman summed up Baby's personality," Mr. Gully continued, "when she told him, 'You have the most indecent eyes of any man I've ever met.' She meant it as a compliment. Baby is not like these rich

Texans whose standard approach is to get a woman drunk. Baby has something money can't buy."

"Would you call Trujillo's son a successful playboy?"

"On the contrary," Mr. Gully said, "I've never met a man who made so many mistakes. He even went on television to announce his courtship to Miss Novak. Can you imagine Baby doing something as idiotic?"

I said I couldn't.

"How long do you keep up a romance?" I asked Mr. Pignatari.

"There is no time limit as long as it's exciting."

"And how do you let the girl down?"

"Any imbecile," he said, "can start a love affair, but it takes a man with a lot of finesse to end it like a gentleman. At the beginning I always warn a girl it's not going to last too long. Then when the time comes there are no surprises. They know I don't want to get married, so they walk in at their own risk."

"Do you give a girl a beautiful present before you say goodbye?"

"He does not," said Mr. Gully. "Baby gives fabulous gifts all during the affair. He's not like most men, who wait until the last minute before they give a girl a present."

"I am very fortunate in that I travel a lot," Mr. Pignatari added. "Travel is always the politest way of ending a romance."

Stamina plays a big part in being a playboy, I discovered. Mr. Pignatari only gets about four hours' sleep a night. Mr. Gully gets five.

Gary Cooper Revisited

I SAW Gary Cooper in Paris.

"Hi," I said.

"Hello, Art. I just came in town with my wife, Rocky, and my daughter, Maria. I just finished a picture in London. Would you like to hear about it?"

"Yup," I said.

"It's an adventure picture about the sea. We had to shoot several scenes in London. They have an important naval hearing in the film in which the facts and responsibilities for the wreck are determined. It was cheaper for Charlton Heston and myself to be brought to London than for the English cast to be flown to Hollywood. Would you like to know who else is in the picture?"

I thought about this for a moment and then said, "Nope."

"Well, would you like to hear about the big water scene?" he said.

"Maybe."

"Charlton Heston and I have an underwater scene in which we fight the villain and his crew. They have underwater spears, and we have nothing except our skin-diving suits. It sounds pretty good, doesn't it?"

"Yup," I agreed.

"I suppose you're wondering what I'm doing in Paris?"

"Nope."

"Well, let me tell you anyway. I'm just vacationing with my wife. I've been working pretty hard lately. Before this picture I made *They Came to Cordura* with Rita Hayworth. It's about an American detachment under Pershing, who is out to find Pancho Villa. I play a major—a coward who is taking back a group of men who have been awarded the Congressional Medal of Honor. I think it's going to be a good picture."

"Could be," I said.

"Would you like to hear my opinions about playing opposite young actresses?"

"Yup."

"Well, I think a man of my age has to be careful about female casting. There were some people who were resentful over the fact I played opposite Audrey Hepburn in *Love in the Afternoon*. Now that admittedly may have been a mistake, but people forget she played opposite Humphrey Bogart in *Sabrina* and there were no complaints about that. The trouble was Audrey looked too young in my picture. She looked about seventeen years old. Maybe it was her hair-do. I think playing against someone who looks seventeen is pretty tough, don't you?"

"Sure."

"I don't have the problem in the *Mary Deare*. The love story isn't that important. It could have been if this was less of a story about the sea and the wreck. On the other hand, Rita Hayworth and I hit it off just fine in *Cordura*. She does a bang-up job in the picture. I think, if I play opposite girls that look over twenty-five I'm all right. It's a funny thing, though. When you play in a Western nobody is bothered by how old the girl is. Of course, when you hit my age you have to have an adult love story. You can't do the standard boy-meets-girl stuff. I know that."

"Uh, huh," I replied.

"I suppose you're wondering what I think about Westerns?"

I didn't say anything.

"Well, they've done everything to kill Westerns in America, but they won't be killed. I thought they'd run out of stories long ago, but apparently they haven't. All they're doing is taking any story that's ever been written and putting it in cowboy dress. It doesn't make any difference if it's *Hamlet* or Pushkin; it eventually winds up as taking place at Bar Z Corral."

"Yup," I said.

"I've been offered many deals to do series for TV, but I don't want to do them.

"I think Westerns should be shot outdoors and look like they take place outdoors. When you reduce them to the size of a television screen, they don't look like much. Do you agree with me?"

"Yup and nope," I said honestly.

"Let me finish," he said. "I'm not against movie Westerns, but every script I've been offered sounds like every previous story I've ever done. I'd like to do a Western, but I think I'd have to produce it myself to make it come out the way I want it to. The trouble is the public likes Westerns whether they're good or bad, so it makes it twice as difficult to make a good one. Do you have any idea where I'm going after Paris?"

"Nope."

"I'm going to the Cap d'Antibes, in the south of France, and do some skin diving. It's a great sport and Rocky and Maria are pretty good at it. We've brought over all our equipment from the United States, and we hope to do some underwater photography. Do you like skin diving?"

"Nope."

"Bird shooting?"

"Nope."

"Are you busy now?"

"Yup."

"That's too bad," Mr. Cooper said sadly. "I rarely get a chance to talk to anybody any more."

He's on Vacation

When I saw Phil Silvers in Paris many years ago he had made his Sergeant Bilko series for television, but they hadn't been released yet. He wasn't too well known at that moment, and I walked around with him for three days without his being recognized. This was pretty hard on his morale, but fortunately on the fourth day we went to lunch at Chez Louis, a sort of Paris Lindy's, and a woman at the next table leaned over and said, "Say, aren't you Phil Silvers?"

For the first time in four days Mr. Silvers smiled, and he said to me, "You see, even in Paris they know me."

During a recent visit to Paris Mr. Silvers had no problem being recognized. For five years as Sergeant Bilko he had been part of the American scene. In London his show was one of the most popular on TV, and everywhere he went he was stopped for autographs.

"I'm fed up with being Sergeant Bilko," Silvers told me in Paris. "I just want to be plain Phil Silvers, tourist. I don't want to give out any more autographs. I'm on vacation. Do you hear? I'm on vacation!"

"Okay, so you're on vacation, and you don't want to sign autographs. You'll have to stay away from the Americans; you'll have to go only where the French people go."

"That's what I want," Silvers agreed. "I want to go where I won't be recognized. I'll leave it to you. I'm in your hands."

The next morning I picked him up and took him to the Musée Henner, a small museum devoted to the drawings of a French artist who is no longer in fashion. There wasn't an American in the museum.

"You're safe here," I told Silvers. "They'll never find you."

"Yeh," agreed Silvers, "that's what I want—obscurity."

From there we went to the Cernuschi Museum, which specializes in Chinese art.

"I can understand no American being here," Silvers said anxiously, "and I can even understand no Frenchman being here. But what I can't understand is why aren't there any Chinese!"

After the Cernuschi Museum I told Silvers I'd take him to a Tunisian restaurant far off the beaten track. I had been with him for three hours, and I thought he'd be pleased that he hadn't met up with any Americans, but he was very glum and unconsciously kept signing his name on the menu. As he dipped into his couscous, he said, "Maybe we ought to stop by the American Express. There might be a letter for me."

"You don't want to go there," I said. "It's full of Americans and they'll drive you crazy. You're on vacation."

"Yeh," he said. "I'm on vacation. I shouldn't forget that."

"After lunch," I promised, "I'll take you to a cement factory on the Seine. Nobody goes there because there is nothing to see."

"You know," he said as we walked through some back alleys, "I think I got a pain in my arm. Maybe I should go the American Hospital and have an American doctor look at it."

"You'll only be mobbed by the patients," I told him. "I'll take you to a French clinic."

"Never mind," he said, "maybe the pain will go away."

We went to a small church in the 20th Arrondissement. Silvers looked disconsolate. "Are there any good American churches we can look at in Paris?"

"There's the American Church and the American Cathedral," I told him, "but there are a lot of tourists in them this time of year, and they'd recognize you in a minute."

"Let's stop by the United States Lines office," he said brightly.

"But you're flying," I said.

"They won't know," Silvers said.

"You'll only wind up with a pen in your hand and a mob around you. Do you want that?"

"Of course not," he said weakly. "I'm on vacation."

We visited a carpet factory on the edge of town and then went to a blacksmith's shop, where Mr. Silvers bought some doorstops. He had to spell his name three times before the man got it.

"Now where do you want to go?"

"I don't know," he said. "Where do you want to go?"

"Wherever you want to go."

"Would it be asking too much of you if we went to Chez Louis?"

"They'll recognize you," I warned.

"I know," said Silvers, "I know."

Something for the Girls

AMONG the successful Americans who have started their own business in Paris is Miss Dorian Leigh, the model. Two and a half years ago Miss Leigh decided that what Paris needed more than anything was a model agency run along American lines. The French government thought otherwise. Thus the battle lines were drawn, and an army of bureaucrats went to battle against one beautiful American girl. You can guess who won.

"Don't say I have a model agency," said Miss Leigh. "Say I've got a bureau des mannequins. That's the way the French police want it. It all started two and a half years ago when I decided I wanted to stay in France and the easiest way of doing it was opening a business—a business I knew something about. In America model agencies are a very common thing, but in France they're unknown. For one thing the Napoleonic Code, which is still the law of the land, says no one may take a percentage of anyone else's salary. Therefore, as an agent, I wasn't allowed to collect a commission from any of the girls I found employment for.

"When I tried to get started I immediately ran head-on

into the Ministry of Labor and the Police, both of whom were very suspicious of my motives. Any time someone gathers a group of girls together for employment purposes in France, the police are bound to think you're up to no good.

"I had several meetings with the authorities. First they didn't believe there were such things as models. They knew of mannequins, but models who posed for pictures were something new to them. I explained that I wanted to start an agency because there was need for a clearing-house for American, German, English, and Scandinavian models who were in demand in France for photography work.

" 'What's the matter with French girls?' the Labor Bureau wanted to know.

"I said, 'I think French girls are the most beautiful girls in the world, but if you go to the Lido or the Casino de Paris you will find, in the front line, English, German, Scandinavian, and even American chorus girls. Why? Because they have long legs and small heads. The French women have short legs and big heads.' I told the authorities photographers wanted girls with long legs and small heads. When I showed them some French fashion magazines and pointed out that a good proportion of the girls were foreign they were staggered.

"Then one of the labor sleuths said, 'I know why. The foreign girls must charge less.' I told him they charged more than French girls. Everyone thought I was off my nut. We finally reached an agreement. I was hired by several French magazines as a fashion consultant. I would supply the models, but instead of taking a commission from them I would take a commission from the one who hired them—either the photographer or the magazine. This seemed to satisfy everyone."

Miss Leigh has fifty-four models working for her, including five men, seven children, and one dog. "I'm always looking for dogs," she said, "but not poodles; they have awful dispositions. I also have trouble finding old ladies. No French woman will admit she's an old lady."

She said that she also represents many French models. "They're the ones that give me gray hair."

"Why is that?" I asked.

"The minute a French girl is born and is told she is beautiful she decides she really doesn't have to do anything.

"The French girls have no ambition when it comes to earning money for themselves. If I have a job for the following evening and I ask a French girl if she wants to go out on it she says, 'I have a dinner date. I can't possibly do it.' If I ask an American model the same question she says, 'How much?' "

Miss Leigh supplies models for many magazine advertisements.

"Occasionally I get a call from an advertiser who wants a model who looks like the typical girl next door. But in France the typical girl next door looks like Brigitte Bardot."

Miss Leigh is newly married to a French obstetrician. "My husband is going out of his mind. He sees women all day long, and when he comes home at night all I talk about is women. He says he's going to take up hunting just so he can see some men again. He must be desperate, because he hates hunting."

Occasionally Miss Leigh gets a call from a businessman

who knows she knows many beautiful girls. "These swine call up and say, 'Joe Blow said I should call. I'm in Paris all by myself and I'm so lonely.' I always reply, 'That's just too bad. Why didn't you bring your wife?' "

A Talk With the Nubam of Lemon

AMONG the distinguished visitors in Rome was the Imam of Yemen, who, as a guest of the Italian government, was traveling with three wives, twenty-six concubines, eight slave girls, and a dozen eunuchs, plus a retinue of fierce, dagger-wielding, scimitar-swinging guards. These figures were given to us by members of the Rome Press Club, and could not be verified by anyone in the Imam's party, because no one was talking. When the Imam arrived in Rome he was put up at a hotel outside of town, but after a news photographer was slashed by one of his guards it was thought best to move him to a more secluded spot at Fregene.

The Imam was being treated in a hospital for various disorders and was not available for comment. It was my hope that I could ask him how it felt to travel with so many women. I find it pretty hard to travel with one wife, and I have nothing but admiration for anyone who can travel with three, not to mention the twenty-six concubines and eight slave girls.

It was my good fortune to run into the bearded Nubam of Lemon, no relation to the Imam, but a big man in his own right. The Nubam is also traveling with the same number of people in his party. He is in Rome for only a few days.

"Your highness," I said, "why are you traveling with three wives, twenty-six concubines, eight slave girls, a dozen eunuchs, and a retinue of fierce, dagger-wielding, scimitar-swinging guards?"

"Because with air travel," he replied in perfect Arabic, "one must travel light. The days of taking a hundred and fifty women on a short weekend to Rome are over.

"Besides, it's getting expensive. A few years ago I could get three hundred rooms for what I'm paying for two hundred rooms now."

"That's true, your Highness, but why do you need three wives with you?"

"Well, *someone* has to pack and unpack you," he replied.

"That's understandable," I agreed. "But why the twenty-six concubines?"

"Look at it this way," he said. "I arrive in Rome with my three wives. One wants to go to the hairdresser, another wants to go shopping, and a third is suffering from food poisoning. What am I supposed to do, sit in my hotel and weave a rug?

"A man can get lonely when he's in Rome," he added, "and I like to be near my family."

"Do you have many problems traveling with so many women?"

"Not any more than the average Nubam. It's the fittings that drive me crazy. Every time we get to Rome everyone, including the slave girls, wants to go out and buy new saris. You can get the same thing for half the price in Lemon, but my women have to have them with a Rome label. As I was just saying to my wives the other day, lemons don't grow on trees. How am I going to pay for all this stuff?"

"What did they say?"

"What any woman would say. They said, 'You knew what we were like when you married all of us.' "

"A typical reaction," I agreed.

"But I'm not complaining," the Nubam said. "For eleven months a year they're stuck in the harem. I'm away a lot on business, so let them have a little fun."

"Do you always travel this way?" I asked.

"Well, actually, I was supposed to come with a friend, but at the last minute he canceled out because sixty-seven of his children were graduating from high school next week. He promised to be at their commencement exercises, and you know how children are if you promise something and don't keep it. Frankly, I'm just as glad he didn't come. It's very hard to travel with other people. My three wives might want to go somewhere, his four wives might want to go somewhere else; I might want to take my concubines to the Opera, he might want to take his to a night club. I think when you're traveling with thirty-seven people you should travel alone.

"It only complicates things if you ask friends along. Now don't get me wrong, I like this guy, but three of his four wives are a pain in the neck. They're always telling my wives how many slaves their husband has. You would think he was the only person in the world with seven hundred million dollars."

"What's your toughest problem?" I asked.

"Taking pictures," the Nubam replied. "Even with a

wide-angle lens I can never seem to get my three wives, twenty-six concubines, eight slave girls, and the Dome of St. Peter's into the same picture."

The Nubam got up. "You'll have to excuse me now," he said. And then, with a wink, he took a black book out of his pocket. "I've got a few good numbers here to call while the girls are out shopping."

Hotels Cost Money

WHAT happens when a billionaire gets tired of living in a hotel? Well, Mr. Paul Getty, America's richest man, went out and bought himself one of those li'l ole stately homes in England. For something like a million dollars Mr. Getty picked up the Duke of Sutherland's famed Sutton Place as well as two hundred of the Duke's seven hundred acres of ground.

It was reported in the newspapers that Mr. Getty bought Sutton Place because he thought it would be cheaper than living in a hotel. When I saw the magnate in London I asked him if it was true.

He said, "Yes."

Which proves once again you can believe everything you read in the newspapers.

Mr. Getty agreed to have a drink with me at the Ritz Hotel in London to tell me about the deal.

"I can't understand what all the fuss is about," he said. "Here I am a tourist, and I just bought an old house in the country, and everyone is talking about it."

Mr. Getty said that he hoped to close the deal the next week so he could move in as soon as possible, because the sooner he moved in, the more money he'd save on the small hotel suite he had at the Ritz.

"Sutton Place is just right for me," Mr. Getty said. "I'm always meeting with business associates, and I can put them up out there far cheaper than I could in a hotel."

"How do you figure that?" I asked him.

"Well, let's look at the problem. You're drinking a tomato juice and I'm drinking a rum and Coca-Cola. Now if you go out and buy the best rum in a store it's not going to cost more than forty shillings ($5.60) a bottle. A Coke shouldn't cost more than sixpence (7 cents). A glass of tomato juice would cost threepence (3½ cents). All right, now we're probably going to get charged seven shillings ($1) for these two drinks.

"We could save four shillings (56 cents) by having this drink at Sutton Place. So you see, living in a hotel does add up. Now let's say you have six people for dinner at home. It shouldn't cost you more than two-fifty a head. But if you had to take the six people to Maxim's it would cost you ten dollars a head."

"At the rate you're figuring," I agreed, "you'll have Sutton Place paid off in no time. But tell me this, Mr. Getty. You own the Hotel Pierre in New York. If you own a hotel like that you can't be very much against hotels."

"Yes, I own the Pierre. But there is no point in using all the money I make in the Pierre staying in other hotels."

"But wait a minute," I said. "Don't forget you're going to have servants at Sutton Place. Don't servants present a problem?"

"Not if you lock everything up and keep the key."

Mr. Getty owns a house on the Persian Gulf, one in Italy, and one in Los Angeles which he hasn't visited since 1951. He keeps a staff of five people in the California home who are supposed to have the house ready on an hour's notice.

"Do you have any plans for charging tourists to visit Sutton Place?"

"No," he said. "I'll leave that to my good friend the Duke of Bedford. I don't want any tourists around. We got a big gate, and they can't get in. The house is a mile away."

"Someone said one of the reasons you decided to move out of a hotel was because you didn't like to tip."

"Well, I'll say this: Tipping is inevitable, but it doesn't add to the joys of living in a hotel."

"Do you think hotels are expensive?"

"Let's say their prices are ambitious. When I spend money I like to get something in return. In a hotel you're throwing your money away. But I'm not going to lose anything by buying Sutton Place. That property is going to be very valuable one of these days."

Another advantage of owning a house in England, Mr. Getty explained, is that you could get a dozen servants in England for what three cost in the United States.

Mr. Getty called for the check. It came to six shillings (eighty-six cents), but the tip wasn't included.

Mr. Getty gave the waiter two shillings more and said to me, "We forgot the tip in our figuring. *Now* do you see what I mean?"

Don't Be a Pal to Your Son

THERE are many different attitudes on how to treat American youth. One I heard comes from Al Capp, the cartoonist, father of three, who told me:

"When I was six years old my parents put me in a clean shirt, pointed out the direction of school, and told me not to come back for eight years. They never expected to see my teachers, and the teachers never expected to see my parents. Each one had a function. My parents were supposed to feed and clothe me; my teacher was supposed to teach me how to read and write. Neither group had any effect on the other. The only thing my parents knew about my teacher was 'she was always picking on me.' Every child's teacher was 'always picking on him.'

"My teachers graded me on arithmetic, English, history, and geography. Since I failed all of them, it was obvious I was going to be a cartoonist. But we were never graded for adjustment, emotional stability, or 'Does he get along with other children?' My parents knew I got along with other children just by virtue of the fact I came home every afternoon with a bloody nose or a black eye.

"In those days we didn't worry about emotional stability. All children were emotionally unstable. They were full of hatreds and frustrations. Wouldn't you be if you were half the size of the rest of the world and didn't have a nickel to your name?

"In my day it wasn't a question of which was the best school to send a kid to, it was which was the nearest one. All schools were good, just as all churches were good and all teachers were good.

"We never heard of words like *adjustment*, *environment*, *rejection*, and *community of children*. Sure we were unloved. We took it for granted that it was natural for everyone to hate us. No one paid any attention to us. And we, in turn, didn't pick up our father's shotgun and wipe out the whole family.

"The child today is wise to the adult jargon, and as soon as he thinks his parents are paying any attention to him the monster swells up in him. The child who is held in proper contempt by his family is grateful for anything he gets. All he needs is food and shelter. If he's loved, he becomes drunk with power, flexes his muscles, and takes over.

"Those parents who concern themselves with their children's problems are crazy. The problems of a nine-year-old kid cannot be solved in any way except by becoming ten. The problems of a sixteen-year-old will only be solved by turning seventeen."

Mr. Capp believes that the emphasis on teen-agers has been damaging. "Teen-agers are repulsive to everybody except each other. We all know that children pass through various stages of insanity, so why try to understand them?"

"But aren't teen-agers unhappy?"

"Sure they are. Let them stay that way. We've put too much emphasis on security. The teen-agers today have been told they have rights. Why should they have rights?

"In Europe kids have no rights. If they ever asked for any they'd get belted by their fathers. But in America, things have been switched around: Children used to try to please their parents—now the parents try to please the children.

"It is my humble belief that we should give American children something they desperately need and crave for—brutality. We must make them feel neglected, insecure, unwanted, and unloved. In return we'll get courtesy, obedience, good scholastic records, and fewer parents will be killed. They'll be so eager to be wanted that they'll do everything in the world to please us."

"Is there anything else?"

"Yes, don't be a pal to your son. Be his father. What child needs a forty-year-old man for a friend? And forget about teaching him the facts of life. There is nothing that a boy could discuss with his father that he couldn't discuss much more openly with his guttersnipe friends.

"Keep in mind we owe children nothing. We'll supply them food, shelter, and clothing only because we're gambling that someday these subhumans will turn into civilized beings and, possibly, make reasonable, honest citizens."

He's Opening Up a Can of Sardines

MR. BILLY WILDER the Hollywood director was touring Europe promoting his film *Some Like It Hot.*

The reaction among European audiences to what has probably been the best farce comedy in years has been excellent, but Mr. Wilder said there is still a small group of

European newspapermen who feel that by his making a successful comedy he has let the whole industry down. "The picture is making a fortune, everyone is laughing, the theaters are crowded, but the question I have to face every morning is, Could this film win first prize at a Yugoslav Film Festival? The answer is probably No, and it bothers me; it really does.

"There is a special technique to making films for a film festival. I've been studying it. Now that I have enough money from this no-message picture I've just made, I'm ready to make a festival picture. I owe it to the critics."

"Do you have a story?" I asked.

"I think I've got one. No one has ever made a film about the plight of the sardine fishermen in the Canary Islands."

"Do they have a plight?"

"They will in my picture. How else will I get it in the festival? The way I visualize it, none of the people have any shoes, and they catch very small sardines."

"Why do they catch very small sardines?"

"Because the Americans won't let the sardines lay the eggs. The villain will be a sardine buyer from A & P who wants to buy up the entire catch. The sardines are much more tasty with eggs in them. But if the sardines can't lay their eggs, there won't be any sardines for the next year.

"The owner of the cannery is in cahoots with the sardine buyer because he's in love with the heroine, and she's in love with the fisherman who wants to save the sardines."

"The picture has everything but symbolism."

"Don't worry, if this picture is going to win at the festival it will have symbolism in it. The people, for example, live three hundred to a house, jammed in together like a can of sardines. The can opener is the symbol of their freedom, and in the final scene the hero stabs the villain with a rusty one he finds on the dock."

"That opens up a new can of sardines," I agreed.

"There is also an attempted-rape scene in the cannery with the owner and the heroine waist-deep in oil. She slips out of his grasp at the last moment and the cannery owner drowns in his own oil."

"It's got realism."

"In the love scene when the hero kisses the heroine I'll cut to a school of sardines mating in a tangled net," Mr. Wilder said.

"The critics will go wild."

"I'll hold the dialogue to a minimum," Mr. Wilder said. "But there is going to be a lot of wind howling. Once in a while I'll go into the local pub and show someone belching."

"I can see the subtitles now."

"There will be no music in the picture except for a Portuguese clavichord, and naturally the picture will be out of focus as if it had been filmed through a thin piece of Roquefort cheese. If you make a picture for a film festival you have to throw out anything that smacks of professional movie-making."

"Whom do you have cast for the picture?"

"Everyone will play himself except the villain, who will be played by Rod Steiger. I would like someone like Spencer Tracy, but after *The Old Man and the Sea*, he refuses to get in a rowboat."

Mr. Wilder said, "The film, even if it wins a prize, may lay an egg at the box office, but if it will help sardines lay their eggs in the Canary Islands I'm willing to sacrifice myself. Those of us who make pictures for film festivals always are."

How To Stop Drinking and Lose Friends

GIVING up the drinking of alcoholic beverages is not as easy as one might think. Thus say Garson Kanin, writer-director, and his wife, Ruth Gordon, writer-actress. The Kanins, at a stone-sober luncheon, told me what they've been through.

"George Jean Nathan," Mr. Kanin told me, "once said, 'I drink to make my friends more interesting.' I stopped drinking because all our friends were disappearing. In 1954 I made four trips up to the Frank E. Campbell Funeral Parlor in New York to bid farewell to contemporaries of mine. As I sat there, while the organ played, and heard their names mispronounced by the hired help, I started to reflect on what brought me and my friend in the box to these unhappy circumstances. In each case I decided drinking played an important part, and finally I reasoned the best thing to do was give it up.

"It was a hard thing to do," Mr. Kanin admitted, "particularly since I liked it so much. My first thought was to drink less, perhaps just wine. But I discovered you can get just as blind on Chablis as you can on whisky."

"We then decided to give it up altogether," Miss Gordon said.

"It isn't difficult to give up drinking," Mr. Kanin said.

"It's just hard to explain it to your friends. At first when you say you've given up drinking your friends laugh at what they think is your little joke and then say, 'That's fine, now what will you have?' If you persist in your refusal they will become nervous, and you can see the mistrust building up. You've let down the team. Overnight you're in the enemy camp; you're either sick or a religious fanatic. Your narrow-minded friends hate you; your understanding friends start speculating on what is the *real* reason you've given it up. If you don't die in six months from a horrible disease then they hate you, too."

"You can take the coward's way out," Miss Gordon said, "and say, when someone offers you a drink, 'Not right now' or 'I'm on a diet' or hold your stomach as if to indicate you've got an ulcer.

"But sometimes it boomerangs. Once I said I had an ulcer and the hostess forced sauerkraut juice on me. Another time the host had a powder which he said permitted him to drink with *his* ulcer. If you open up your stomach to somebody, they'll open theirs to you."

"Once you've stopped drinking you're subject to dictums," Mr. Kanin said. "The one I've heard time and time again is quoted from the Yale School of Alcoholic Studies and is 'Drink if you want to; don't drink if you have to.' Now this is a real trap, because it means if you turn down a drink it's obvious you're an alcoholic.

"Another theory your friends express, when they're drunk, of course, is that the reason you don't drink is because you're trying to save money. You're just a stingy miserly s.o.b. in their eyes and antisocial to boot. But you don't save money when you don't drink. For one thing, to keep the few friends you've got, you have to serve them liquor at home. For another, you're usually so bored in a bar or a cabaret listening to your pals getting stinko that you're the first one to call for the check. And for a third thing, you're so afraid of bartenders and wine stewards that you tip far more for drinking nonalcoholic drinks than alcoholic ones.

"When I used to drink I never did such an inconceivable thing as call for the check."

"The thing friends say to you when you announce you've given up drinking," Miss Gordon said, "is 'Do you miss it?' At first we used to reply, 'No, we don't miss it at all.' But after we lost six friends this way we changed our line, and now when we're asked if we miss it we reply, 'We don't see how we can get through another day without it.' "

At cocktail parties the Kanins have learned certain basic tricks. They are never caught without glasses in their hands—water and ice if they're pretending to drink vodka; ginger ale if they're pretending to drink whisky.

"Never accept a drink from your host if you have no intention of drinking it," Mr. Kanin warned me. "If you don't drink it, he'll think you're criticizing his liquor."

The Kanins estimated they had four close friends who considered them eccentrics but were willing to put up with them after they gave up drinking. "But then," Mr. Kanin said sadly, "we gave up smoking and now we've lost all of them."

Ireland's Enfant Terrible

BRENDAN BEHAN, the *enfant terrible* of the Irish literary world, was in Paris for the opening of his play *The Quare Fellow.* Mr. Behan, whose book *Borstal Boy* was a best-seller in England and the United States, was a hard man to see. In the morning he was suffering from a hangover, and in the afternoon and evening he was in the process of preparing himself for the hangover of the next morning.

I met Mr. Behan at high noon at his hotel. He was wearing a blue tie. "I wear a red tie for my school," he told me, "a green tie for my country, and a blue tie when I have a hangover. I have been partial to blue lately."

Mr. Behan is thirty-six years old. Three of these years were spent in Borstal Reform School, England, for being involved with the Irish Republican Army. Another four were spent in an Irish prison (1942–1946) for the attempted murder of two detectives. Mr. Behan was released in a general amnesty in 1946, but was arrested again in 1947, this time in Manchester, for having assisted in the escape of an IRA man. He got four months for that.

It was obvious Mr. Behan had never had warm feelings toward the police.

"I am not fond of the police anywhere. In Ireland or in France or in England either. I have heard no good reports about the New York police, though most of them are of Irish descent. Nor have I heard anything nice about the Russian or the German police.

"I find policemen are peasants who are delighted to be let loose in uniforms with guns through the very streets they crawled in dumb, wondering fear when first they left the bog. It is not their fault. Lenin said the aim of all politics was the abolition of the village idiot. The world being a madhouse, who is more fitting to patrol its wards than armed idiots?

"No decent writer could have affection for the police. They are on the side of power; we are on the side of liberty."

Mr. Behan had had several minor scrapes with the French police. Once he made a row out at Orly about getting on an airplane. He had a dread of flying. "I was very disturbed by the newspaper reports of that incident," he said. "The newspapers quoted me as saying I did not want to die for France. This made it sound like I was anti-French. What I actually said was, "I do not want to die for Air France."

The writer said he had a warm spot in his heart for France. He had lived here several years working as a house painter.

"The French are not hypocrites," he said. "You can smash up a pub, and as long as you pay the damage you're welcome to do it on the same terms the next evening."

At that moment, Mr. Behan estimated, he was banned from about fourteen pubs, mostly in London and Dublin. He blamed his trouble on his fondness for Irish whisky and Guinness stout.

"I don't necessarily drink them together," he said, "but there is a very short interval between them. In Dublin, during the depression when I was growing up, drunkenness was not regarded as a social disgrace. To get enough to eat was regarded as an achievement; to get drunk was a victory."

Mr. Behan's book *Borstal Boy*, which is about his adventures in prison, has been banned in Ireland. He thinks it's mainly because of what he wrote about the Catholic chaplains there.

"My father was excommunicated in 1922 as a Republican and in 1939. But it doesn't trouble anyone in Catholic countries, the priest least of all. If you are getting married or buried, he'll be there. I'm a bad Catholic, like many greater artists. It is my hope, however, that the Church's information about the next world is more accurate than her views on this one. Otherwise the bad may suffer with the good for eternity.

"Before *Borstal Boy* was banned it was on sale for two weeks, and many priests I know managed to get copies. They told me they liked it, and one priest wrote to me and said it should be sent to every prison chaplain in the world."

I asked him how he felt about being a successful writer.

"I think everyone should be successful for one month. But that's all. The trouble with being successful is, people always want to buy you drinks, and then the hangovers become bigger all the time. When I was a house painter in Paris I drank only red wine. I never had hangovers such as I have now.

"I would like to visit the United States some time, but I understand that the hospitality is so overwhelming there, all of it hard liquor, that I fear I might come home in a box."

Another reason for Mr. Behan's distrusting success, he

said, was that he felt "the police pick you up faster when you become well known. I guess they want to cash in on the publicity."

I asked Mr. Behan if he was married.

"Yes, I am," he said, "to a very dear girl who is an artist. We have no children—except me."

A New Credit-Card Club

I GOT to talking about credit cards recently with Herb Sargent, a television writer. Mr. Sargent told me there are credit cards for almost everything now. The Diners' Club, the Esquire Club, the American Express Club, and many others are issuing cards by the millions for people traveling abroad. It's almost un-American these days to pay for anything in cash.

Unfortunately there are still some places where the existing credit cards are no good, and to fill the gap, Mr. Sargent is starting his own Sargent Credit Club.

For a five-dollar membership fee Mr. Sargent will issue a book of perforated tickets. This will give the tourist credit for such things as the Trevi Fountain in Rome. Up until now people who want to come back to Rome have thrown coins into the Trevi Fountain. With Mr. Sargent's credit system all you have to do is tear off a ticket and throw it into the fountain. You can then charge it off on your taxes to wishful thinking.

The book, which is not transferable, also has tickets for St. Mark's Square in Venice. Instead of buying a bag of corn to feed the pigeons, the club member tears up a ticket (worth fifty cents, or one dollar if he really likes pigeons) into little pieces and sprinkles it among the birds.

In some ports in the Mediterranean and off the Hawaiian Islands tourists are expected to throw coins off the ships to children who dive for them. Mr. Sargent has perfected a specially weighted ticket which the children can dive for and redeem, less Mr. Sargent's 7 per cent commission.

Mr. Sargent believes there are many people who don't want to hang down and kiss the Blarney Stone in Ireland. All a tourist with his credit card has to do is lower the card by a string, and he will be credited with kissing the stone.

Mr. Sargent's card also provides for robbery abroad. If a cardholder is held up in a foreign city, he does not turn over his cash but produces his credit card. The stick-up man takes down the number and sends in the bill directly to Mr. Sargent, depending on how much he thought the tourist had on him at the moment. This does away with mugging and violence and keeps robberies at a civilized level. If the stick-up man is rude or uses abusive language, Mr. Sargent will take him off his accredited list, and the stick-up man will not be allowed to hold up any other Sargent Club members.

One of the great advantages Mr. Sargent's organization has over other credit organizations is that there are many people who don't want to go abroad but feel they should. For these people Mr. Sargent has arranged that they can send their credit cards abroad without themselves.

The credit card is put on a boat and is met at the dock by a liveried chauffeur and Cadillac. A guide registers it in a hotel, where it spends the night. In the morning another guide takes it on a tour of the city, and so on for the duration of the trip.

There is an extra charge if the card goes somewhere that is not on the tour.

One of the highlights of the tour is that if you send the credit card to the Café de la Paix it will see every other validated credit card in the world.

By sending the credit card alone you don't save money, but you avoid all the inconveniences of traveling, and in the winter you can say to friends, "Would you like to see what our trip to Europe cost us this year?"

Mr. Sargent also has economy tours. If you can find twelve people who don't want to go abroad at the same time, he will send all the credit cards together and everyone saves 20 per cent.

Mr. Sargent has utmost faith in his club.

"There are still some people in the United States who insist on paying cash for everything," he told us. "But they're slowly dying out, mostly of malnutrition, because they can't get a meal in a restaurant or groceries delivered to their homes.

"Some have tried to leave the country, but no airline or boat would book them, and no hotel would take them."

"Why not?"

"If they paid cash, no one would know what their credit rating was. How would you know if they were a good risk or not?"

4. "The Irrational Set"

A Discussion of Rich People

My friend Thornton Wilder invited me out for a fondue at St. Moritz.

"I know what I'm doing here," I told him, "but what are you doing here?"

"I am writing seven one-act plays on the seven deadly sins."

"Isn't this a dangerous place to work?"

"You can find many of the sins right here in St. Moritz. Of course one mustn't overdo it. I've made it a principle to work five days and then break out on the sixth, tearing up a few St. Moritz cobblestones along the way."

"You're probably the only writer in the Engadine Valley. Don't you find yourself out of place?"

"I'm not a social climber, but I discovered that if you disappear for five days at a time your reappearance on the sixth day is strangely welcome. It's the tragedy of those who live entirely for pleasure that they congregate in resorts where they see each other twenty times a day. A new face is always a welcome relief.

"Besides, I don't feel out of place. A writer's business is to have his eyes rest on as many human beings as possible. I have stayed in the motels of America and have been rewarded with many wonderful encounters.

"From time to time I find myself among the very rich, such as here at St. Moritz. The proportion is the same of hopeless, self-destructive waste as against amiable contacts and lovable, rewarding human beings. I have never believed that poverty totally destroys, nor that wealth totally corrupts.

"But, Archie, we must differentiate between those who have wealth and those who live for pleasure. Unhappily, those who live for pleasure are always looking over their shoulders in hopes of finding the pleasure somewhere else.

"The two greatest laws of mankind are that man is in the world to make something new, and woman is in the world, for the most part, to serve him who makes something new. If a man is rich and unproductive he's out of relationship with the universe, and since the women about him have nothing to contribute, a strange, febrile diversion takes place.

"The rich in the past were not burdened with the problem of productivity. In other centuries they had an inner, mystic feeling that they were God's children, and no one questioned it.

"But in the twentieth century the mystic is gone, and birth and privilege are disappearing. No matter how much money they have, they have to be reassured, mainly by the newspapers and magazines, that they are somebody.

"The rich may claim to detest the press, but without the reassurance of the society pages and columns that they are what they think they are, they would have a completely empty feeling in their stomachs, and it would be impossible for them to know if other people thought them precious."

"Then the rich need the press more than we need them?" I asked hopefully.

"I would certainly say so. Of course, one of the pleasures of the rich is to corrupt the press."

"How can I avoid being corrupted?"

"You could pay for your own drinks."

"That's going a bit far," I protested.

"And you might pay for your own dinners."

"I'd rather be corrupted."

"But most of all, don't let them flatter you. The worst type of corruption for a newspaperman is flattery."

"I'll drink their drinks, and I'll eat their food, but I won't let anyone flatter me," I vowed. "The next person who says I'm a good polo player will get a piece of my mind."

A Survey in Switzerland

WHAT a glorious month February 1959 was for Switzerland! On the first of February the Swiss electorate rejected a proposal to allow women to vote in federal elections by 654,924 to 323,306. Only three cantons out of twenty-two —Geneva, Neuchâtel, and Vaud—voted for women's suffrage.

As European representative of the recently revived Bull Moose party, an American organization whose sole purpose is to keep women from voting, I could take personal pleasure in the victory. Telegrams and letters of congratulations have been pouring in from all over the world and even the executive committee of the Bull Moosers in New York were pleased. Their telegram said: "HEARTIEST CONGRATULATIONS ON SWISS VICTORY STOP PLEASE GIVE FULLEST DETAILS AS WELL AS WHAT MISTAKES WERE MADE IN GENEVA NEUCHATEL AND VAUD SO IT WON'T HAPPEN AGAIN STOP STRIKE WHILE THE FONDUE SIMMERS."

In order to find out what really happened in Switzerland I decided to select a typical Swiss village and make a study of the situation. I chose a little town in the Engadine Valley called St. Moritz, as typical a Swiss village as you can find anywhere. Here, hidden in the Alps, you will find such old Swiss names as Elsa Maxwell, Stavros Niarchos, Tina Onassis, Arturo Lopez, Tex Feldman, Gianna Angelli, Count Theo Rossi, Mrs. Serge Semenenko, Princess Soraya, and Sir Gordon Richards.

St. Moritzers have always guarded their females, and although the women no longer wear veils, they keep their ski-boot laces tied very tight.

I stepped into the village bar in the Palace Hotel to talk to a few of the natives.

The natives, all dressed in black tie and evening gowns, were spending a typical evening gossiping about the day's events as they do in every village in Switzerland.

One man said, "I don't care how much oil tankers cost in France; I'm not going to pay more than $16,900,000 for the boat and that's final."

The lady at the next table said, "My favorite dish is baked potato and caviar. It has both the taste of the earth and the sea."

The man with her said, "I told you not to wear those jewels until I got them insured."

"I beg your pardon," I said. "Could you tell me why Switzerland voted against women's suffrage?"

"Switzerland?" The man looked up. "Where the hell is that?"

I tried another table. "I don't care what you say," someone was saying, "I think snow tires on a Bentley look ugly."

I asked a man, "Would you want your wife to vote in a secret ballot?"

"She does everything else behind my back; I guess her voting would be the least of my troubles."

"What kind of voting is the man talking about?"

"I think he's talking about voting someone into the Corviglia Ski Club."

"It can't be done," a man huffed. "Too many members now. I'll complain to the secretary about it in the morning."

A beautiful blonde walked across the room.

"Would you like to vote?" I asked her.

"Not to this music," she replied, "but try me later."

I finally got one man at the bar to admit he was against women voting. "I'm against women having the right to vote," he said. "A woman's place is on her yacht with her children."

It was five o'clock in the morning, and, as in most Swiss villages, the crowd in the bar was thinning. I discovered it isn't as easy to discuss women's suffrage in St. Moritz as I thought it would be. The Swiss are a close-mouthed people, and apparently they don't like to talk politics with strangers.

A Promise Made Is, Etc., Etc.

THE Swiss mountains were getting me down and so I put in for a transfer to Monte Carlo.

"Why don't you go alone?" my wife said.

"It wouldn't be any fun alone," I said, flushing with excitement. "But then again it hardly seems fair to drag you and the children away from this paradise."

"You need the rest," she insisted. "Besides, you didn't bring a raincoat here and we did."

"Well, as long as you put it that way, I'll just make a fast trip down there to take a swim, and I'll be back before the snow melts on the Matterhorn."

"All right," she said, accepting a pair of pearl earrings as a gift. "But promise me you won't talk to any single woman."

"I won't even talk to married women," I promised. "You don't have to worry about me."

Before she could change her mind, I was on a plane to Paris and then on the Blue Train to Monaco.

The Blue Train arrives in Cannes at eight o'clock, in Nice at eight thirty, and in Monte Carlo at nine thirty. The train was full when I left Paris, but, by the time I arrived in Nice, there were only two of us left in the car. Besides myself there was an attractive woman who seemed to be traveling all alone. As the train pulled out of Nice, both of us were standing in the aisle looking out the window.

She smiled at me, but I didn't smile back.

"Everybody got off the train," she said.

I didn't reply.

"It's so lonely."

I turned the other way.

"Are you going to Monte Carlo?"

I nodded yes.

"So am I."

I smiled.

"Traveling can get to be so lonely. Have you ever had the feeling you want to talk to somebody in the worst way?"

"Once in a while," I said, breaking the silence, "but not very often."

"I love to talk to people, but very few people talk to me."

I didn't say anything.

"I have a wonderful story to tell someone."

I pretended I was trying to close the window.

"It's filled with sadness and loneliness," she continued. "But no one will listen to it."

I got the window closed.

"Would you believe it, you're the first stranger I've wanted to talk to in thirty years?"

I opened the window.

"I guess I've always been frightened of people."

We went into a tunnel.

When we came out she said, "You have a sympathetic face. Would you listen to my story?"

I shook my head.

The silence was embarrassing.

"Wouldn't you even listen to part of it?"

I shook my head again.

"One small anecdote?"

I shook my head again.

"That's the trouble," she sighed. "When I finally meet someone I want to talk to, he doesn't want to listen."

I wanted to explain to her the promise I made to my wife, but she wouldn't have understood. Instead I said, "I want to be alone," and went back into my own compartment to read the newspaper.

When I arrived in Monte Carlo there was only one porter and I had to share him with the lady. As I got to the gate, I saw a friend of mine, George Schlee, run up to the woman and kiss her.

Then he shook hands with me, and said, "I see you've met Greta."

"Greta who?" I said, turning to the woman.

"Greta Garbo."

I threw myself in front of the next train going back to Paris.

Sometimes It's Very Tough

ONE of the tough things about this job is that many times I have to go on assignments without my wife. Although I'm always pointing out that it's the husband's job to hunt for food while the wife stays protecting her cubs, it never seems to ease the tension at the time of parting.

One weekend I had to go to Monaco to attend a gala Frank Sinatra was giving to launch his film, *Kings Go Forth.* It was very important for me to go. First, Frank Sinatra doesn't usually invite newspapermen to anything, much less a gala. Secondly, it was an important social event, and finally, the trip was free.

I tried to point out to my wife that not only would it be important for my prestige as a columnist to attend (Earl Wilson, Bob Considine, Leonard Lyons, and Louis Sobol were all going to be there.), but I would actually be saving money, because for three days United Artists was going to pay for all my meals.

"Go ahead," she said. "I don't mind staying home while you go to Monte Carlo. We all have our work to do."

"That's what I call an understanding wife," I said, throwing my suitcase in the air. "I'll rush back as soon as it's over. I hate these trips as much as you hate my taking them. Damn people like Frank Sinatra. Why can't they let us live in peace?"

"Don't forget your bathing suit," she said bitterly. "You might want to interview someone in the swimming pool."

I threw the swim suit back into the closet.

"Swimming! Are you kidding? I'll be lucky to get out of my hotel room to take a bath."

The gala was Saturday evening, and I vowed I'd call my wife the first thing Sunday morning. The first thing Sunday morning happened to be around one o'clock in the afternoon. With my head throbbing from champagne, I called Paris.

A brave, cold voice was on the other end of the line.

"How was the gala?" she asked.

"How are all galas?" I replied. "It was just another gala."

"Did you have any fun?" The voice was ten degrees colder.

"It depends on what you call fun. If you think eating smoked salmon, foie gras, chicken in aspic, strawberries and ice cream, and drinking a bottle of champagne in a crowded hot room is fun, then I had fun. But you were lucky you didn't come."

"Why?" she wanted to know.

"You know Monaco as well as I do. Nothing but women

and jewels and all the girls showing off their new clothes, and people going swimming at all hours of the night. It's a regular rat race. You would have hated every minute of it."

"Who was at the gala?"

"Princess Grace and Prince Rainier, Frank Ross and Joan Caulfield, Mr. Onassis, and a few other people. Nobody really knew anybody."

"Did Frank sing?"

"Yeah, he sang. Maybe for an hour or so. But outside of that there wasn't much to do but dance and talk to people."

"What time did you get to bed?"

"Early. Maybe four thirty or five in the morning. Sinatra wanted us to keep him company. It was a small party up in his room, but you wouldn't have known any of the people. I kept wanting to go to sleep but you know how Sinatra is. He wanted all of us to watch the sunrise from his room. Harry Kurnitz says he's the only person who invites you to a black-tie dinner and tells you to bring sunglasses."

"So you stayed up to watch the sunrise?" Her voice sounded as if it were coming from a deepfreeze.

"Yeah. It was a lousy sunrise. I thought the sun would never get up."

"What are you going to do today?"

"I've got to go out and buy a bathing suit. There is some English starlet who said that I could have an exclusive interview with her, and I thought it would be clever if I interviewed her by the swimming pool. But really I'm sorry I came. You were so right when you said there wasn't much here for me to do. I could have got the whole story from the wire services."

"What are you doing tonight?"

"Tonight's the worst of all. Somebody is giving us a party on a yacht. It sounds terrible. I hope it rains."

Our Leading Hostess

(While I was on vacation I asked Elsa Hogenblatt, well-known party-giver, hostess, and international society queen to tell us, in her own words, about her interesting life.)

As THE world's leading society hostess, I am constantly being asked for the recipe of my success. Why is it that more people—titled people, people with money and influence, people who should know better—are always asking me to throw parties, go on cruises, visit their palaces, join them in Biarritz, Monte Carlo, and Venice? I'm not as beautiful as Truman Capote, I'm not as rich as Orson Welles, and I'm not as young as Gary Cooper. And yet, when someone raises a flag they always want to know if "Elsa is going to salute."

Why am I always in demand? I must have something nobody else has. But what is it?

Just the other day the Duchess of Whimpers said to me, "Elsa, the Duke is going to have his tonsils out next week and we both want you to be on the operating table with us."

This is happening to me all the time. Naturally, I've accepted. The duchess is a most attractive person and sets a lovely table.

Last month the Eli Kahn, who is one of my dearest friends and owns a wonderful stable of horses, said to me,

"Elsa, my horse Starkweather has thrown a shoe and I won't be able to enter him in the Grand Prix at Longchamp. I was wondering if you would run in his place." Naturally, I accepted. I love Longchamp and you can see so much more when you're in the race yourself. I didn't win, but Eli said I ran a good race, and on the basis of it he's invited me to Ascot next year.

I don't know why people are always seeking me out. Take last week, for example. I was down on the Riviera trying to decide which yacht to go on when my dear friend Stavros Carcuss, the Nepalese Shipping Millionaire, called me and said, "Elsa, my Chris-Craft is stuck in the sand. Would you mind coming over and pulling it out for me?" That's the way Stavros is, always inviting me to something. Well, as much as I hate to be tied down, I was, and I pulled the boat off the sand in no time.

If I had to sum up in one word why I'm so much in demand, I would say it was because I love "fun." I could have fun if I was a defendant in the Lacaze case. The doctors say it has something to do with my joie de vivre.

The only thing I hate is riffraff. I can forgive a person anything, except if he doesn't have a title or money.

Last year when I was staying with the King and Queen of Upper Gesundheit they said to me, "Elsa, the people are complaining because they have no bread!"

I said to the King and Queen, "Tell them to eat cake."

They liked the remark so much, they lost their heads over it. But that's the way I am, frank and to the point.

It goes without saying I give the best parties in the world. Everybody wants to go to my parties. I don't know why. I just gave a party for Pia Callous, the great Yemenite opera star who was treated so badly by Mr. Bing at the Metropolitan Opera House because she had a sore throat.

But my party made up for it, and anyone who was anyone was invited.

It was the most successful of the year. Miss Callous sang for us, and all she had to do was open her mouth and *everyone* went home with a sore throat.

People are always saying to me, "Elsa, how can you throw such parties on the eighty-dollar social security you get each month?"

I always reply you don't need money to have good parties. All you need is wonderful people like the Duchess of Whimpers, Eli, Stavros, Pia, and someone to call for separate checks.

Some Call It Fasching

EVERYWHERE in Europe there are folk festivals celebrating some historical event in the locality's past. Munich, Germany, is no exception. As a matter of record, Munich has more celebrations than it has historical events. The longest, the wildest, the most dangerous, the most tiring, and the *most* festive is called Fasching, which is celebrated without letup from January seventh until Ash Wednesday. It is such an old festival that no one knows exactly what he's celebrating. Most Munichers claim it originally had something to do with fertility rites, and if it didn't, it should have.

It is very hard to describe Fasching to someone who is not on the scene. And if you're on the scene it's very hard to describe anything.

While other cities have their Mardi Gras carnivals preceding Lent, Munich is the city that celebrates most all through the pre-Lent period. About two thousand balls are held throughout the city, not to mention eight thousand smaller parties. The balls, which start around ten o'clock in the evening, have to last, by law, until dawn. The majority of them are masquerade balls, and it is not uncommon to see people on streetcars and in the main squares of this city in wild, often immodest, costumes, going to or from a party.

Each profession gives its own ball. The policemen have a ball; the hairdressers have a ball; the streetcar conductors have a ball; the journalists, the lawyers, the export managers, the college students, the teen-agers, the sub-teenagers—and even newborn babies at the maternity hospitals have a ball. No one can escape balling during the Fasching season.

Naturally, when one of the unions has its ball, there is a noticeable drop in the service involved the next morning. If, for instance, the police have their ball, the next morning the traffic situation serves as a barometer as to how successful the party was. If it's completely tied up, everyone in Munich knows the police had a good time. On another evening, the postal workers' ball will definitely affect mail distribution for a few days.

But I'm digressing. I arrived late on Monday night and some friends had arranged to take me to my first Fasching ball. I looked forward to it with as much enthusiasm as I did to the first time I was getting a pair of long pants. Unfortunately all the stores were closed and I needed a costume to get into the ball. My friend said, "Do you have a tuxedo?"

I said I did.

"Put it on; I will lend you my top hat. I have an idea."

When I got to the ball I was stopped at the door.

"You must have a costume," the doorman said.

"He has a costume," my friend said.

"What is he going as?" the doorman asked.

"He's going as an unpunished war criminal."

And sure enough I was allowed to go inside.

(*Would the man who asked me to dance with his wife so he could dance with a blonde two nights ago please reclaim her in the cloakroom of the Regina Hotel?*)

Where should I start? Well, in order to give you some idea of how wild Fasching gets in Munich, I will give you a run-down on the children's party which was held recently at the Hotel Bayrischer Hof. It was called the Kindermaskenball in der Prinzenresidenz and was open to children aged two to ten. From this ball you can get some idea of what the adult balls are like. The Kindermaskenballs are the children's training grounds for Fasching, somewhat like our Little Leagues are for baseball in America.

(*Will the lady who left her costume in my rented car please reclaim it at the Hertz Drive-It-Yourself Agency?*)

There must have been over five hundred children in the decorated ballroom. There were masked cowboys, Indian maharajas, veiled Fatimas, blonde angels, green devils, wild and domestic animals (one little boy came as half a horse, as his brother, who was supposed to be the other half, had come down with a cold), clowns, ballet dancers, bathing beauties, and sexy chorus girls.

At the beginning of the party, which started at three in the afternoon, everyone was very well-behaved (this is true at the beginning of all Fasching parties). The orchestra played waltzes and fox trots, and girls danced with girls, except for a few who had been forced to dance with their brothers. There were also many five- and six-year-olds who were dancing by themselves.

(*Will the lady who gave me her telephone number and told me to call her any afternoon before five send it to me again? The number she gave me belongs to the Bavarian Road Repair and Highway Commission.*)

But as the carnival wore on it started to get wild. A Turkish sultan tripped a Madame Butterfly and she started crying. The mother of the Turkish sultan whacked him, and he started to cry. In a corner, a four-year-old Swiss yodler was shoving confetti down the mouth of his two-year-old sister, and in another corner three cowboys and a white hunter were shooting two little girls dressed in leopard skins. In still another corner a masked prince was wrestling with a cave man while their mothers were trying to get them to eat their cream pies. In the meantime the orchestra had switched to rock 'n roll, and the floor was covered with screaming, jumping, hysteric bodies. Chairs were overturned, chorus girls disappeared under tables, naval officers cried for ice cream, and two Arab chiefs (about seven and eight years old) stretched out on the dance floor and refused to move.

All in all it was a pretty successful Fasching ball, and from this you can get some idea of what the adult Fasching balls are like, only more so.

(Will the American army officer's wife who said she was coming to Paris next week to continue the Fasching season when it was over in Munich forget the whole thing? I was only kidding.)

And after the teachers' ball, school children more or less have the classrooms to themselves.

The important thing to remember, and the thing I haven't been allowed to forget, is that a good Municher or a friend of Munich, or even someone just driving through on his way to Vienna, is expected to attend at least three balls an evening. One cannot go to a mannequins' ball without also going to the Sanitation Department's ball. If one goes to the ball of the butchers he wouldn't be getting all his proteins unless he also attended the vegetable-sellers' ball.

Since this is the shortest Fasching season (only thirty-six days) in the memory of many Fasching people (the average runs between sixty and ninety days without letup), everyone has doubled his (or her) efforts to make it as gay as possible. The people are working at it harder, and they're living it up as if there were no tomorrow, a very foolish thing in my opinion, since in Munich there is always tomorrow, and another ball to go with it.

I hope I'm not giving the impression that just because people stay up all night every night for thirty-six nights, they don't go to work the next day. They do go to work the next day, but that's where most of them sleep.

As the season draws to an end, Munichers get wearier and wearier, and it is at this moment that German businessmen from other parts of Germany move in for what they hope will be a killing.

At the same time Fasching is the perfect excuse in a

Munich courtroom for any crime involving a man and a woman, not necessarily married or even near it.

If either mate goes astray during this period, and it's doubtful that even Lloyd's of London will insure against it, the matter is laughed away and both parties usually promise to be faithful to each other until Oktoberfest, which starts on the last day of September and lasts for two weeks.

The Factory

NESTLED on the coast of Normandy within Rolls Royce distance of Paris, a precious stone's throw from Havre as the chinchilla flies, is the tiny town of Deauville. Surrounded by jewelry stores, steeped in thoroughbred horseflesh, rolling in French poodles, Deauville owes its popularity to one of the greatest casinos in Europe, and because of it everyone here owes something to the casino.

Unlike the Riviera, where a man's wealth is judged by how many guests he can get to his villa or on his yacht, Deauville has little social life outside of the casino and the race track. We who went there for the summer season went to avoid the chi-chi that has become so common in the rest of France. All you need to belong in Deauville is a bathing suit, suntan oil, the inner tube of a rubber tire, and a string of polo ponies. The rest is up to you.

The difference between Deauville and other resorts is that the people who go there don't go for fun. It's true in the daytime they relax on the beach, take a flyer at the track, or sit in the hairdresser's waiting for night to fall, but in the evening everyone has to go to work. Both men and women dressed in overalls pour forth from their dormitories to head for a large, baroque, white building which is known as the "factory." The factory is owned by a benign eighty-year-old man named François André. M. André makes only one product—money. But this product has been so much in demand in France that M. André has been able to keep between one thousand and two thousand people busy every evening. No one who sincerely wants to work has ever been turned away.

The factory is laid out like a gambling casino. There are three large halls filled with tables and chairs. There are no time clocks in the factory. When a worker arrives he hands in a sheet of thin paper which is called francs. In exchange he is given a pile of plastics called chips. When the worker uses up all the plastics he is allowed to go home.

Some experienced workers can use them up in less than an hour. Others dawdle and goof off and it sometimes takes them all night to use them up.

There are different kinds of work in the factory. At some tables the workers sit at a green felt-covered table. In the center is a wheel and a white ball. The table is covered with numbers and the workers place their plastic chips on the numbers. Then the foreman spins the wheel and the white ball goes whirling around. As soon as it falls into a numbered hole, M. André has made his money.

As in any factory, there are accidents, and once in a while the white ball falls into a hole on a number corresponding to the one on which the worker has just placed his plastic chips. In this case he is penalized by being given thirty-five plastic chips for every one he placed on the number. This is M. André's method of punishing the worker for his carelessness, because the more plastic chips a person has, the longer he has to remain in the factory.

Carelessness is one thing M. André can't stand.

At other tables workers sit sorting cards, and everything here is done by hand.

The really skilled workers sit at these tables and M. André takes personal pride in the fine work these people do for him.

Needless to say, M. André doesn't run a sweatshop (except on gala evenings in the ballroom when Edith Piaf is brought up from Paris to entertain the people), and working conditions are very pleasant. There are bars, several working-class restaurants where for ten dollars you can get a box lunch with a bottle of champagne, a golf course, and three large dormitories called the Normandy, Royal, and Golf where most of the workers sleep.

Unlike Monte Carlo, the suicide rate in Deauville is very low because it's so hard to get a room here, and once you've got it, you hate to give it up.

5. “Gaîté Parisienne”

She Wants To Get Married

I HAVE a secretary named Ursula. She is a Swiss girl, and in the eyes of the French, a foreigner. This hasn't bothered Ursula in the past, but recently she's been trying to get married to a Frenchman and it isn't as easy as it sounds.

In order for a foreigner to get married in France, one must get, among other things, permission from the Prefect of Police. No one is quite sure why you must have police permission except that everything official in France usually begins and ends at the police station.

Ursula started out two and a half months ago to get the permission, and as a disinterested spectator, I've been watching the course of events with interest.

My secretary first had to make application at her town hall in the 16th Arrondissement. She needed four papers, they told her: her birth certificate, her certificate of domicile, a certificate from her doctor, and, last but not least, authorization from the police.

Ursula went down to the main police station on the Ile de la Cité and made an application for authorization to get married. Thirty minutes later the woman behind the counter returned to tell Ursula that the authorization could not be given immediately because in 1956 she had changed apartments without telling the police. There is no more serious crime in France (unless you can prove it was a crime of passion) than moving in France without telling the Prefect. And Ursula was informed she would have to be investigated.

The woman behind the counter said the investigation would be held by the commissariat in Auteuil where Ursula lived, and the papers would be sent there. Ursula cried, but the woman said she should come back in two weeks.

Ten days later Ursula received a summons to go to the commissariat on Friday at seven o'clock at night.

Ursula arrived promptly at seven and waited.

At five of eight she was informed that the person who was to interview her was off on Fridays and she had better come back on Saturday at two in the afternoon. At two Ursula found herself with a mob of people trying to get passports to go on vacations. When her turn finally came to be called to the desk everyone in the crowded office could listen in. She was questioned at length about her business and personal life, and then the man said she could go home.

"But what about the authorization of marriage?" Ursula asked.

"I don't know about any authorization of marriage," the man replied. "I don't even know why I'm questioning you. I was just told to question you and I did."

Two weeks later Ursula went to the Préfecture for her authorization. No one there knew anything about it. The file, they said, was at the commissariat, so it wasn't their concern. They suggested she come back in two weeks. If nothing happened in two weeks, they suggested she start all over again.

Ursula went from the Préfecture to the commissariat. She asked them why they hadn't forwarded her papers to

the Préfecture. They replied they had forwarded them three weeks previously.

"But," Ursula said, "you only questioned me two weeks ago."

"Well," said the man, "if that's all it was, what are you complaining about?"

Besides, the man in the commissariat said, the people in the Préfecture are the ones who lose things, not the commissariat.

Ursula took a taxi back to the Préfecture. The woman behind the counter told her not to believe everything the commissariat told her. She had received no papers yet.

Suddenly Ursula got a bright idea and she leaned over the counter and whispered in the woman's ear.

It was what women have been whispering to each other ever since time began. "If my mother finds out before we're married," Ursula said tearfully, "she will never forgive me."

The woman looked down at Ursula's stomach. "But it is not serious yet," she said. "You still have time."

Ursula cried some more and the woman said, "All right. I will mark your application 'Urgent.' Come back in two weeks."

Two weeks later Ursula stuffed a scarf underneath her dress and returned. The papers weren't ready, but the woman, after seeing Ursula's condition, marked in the application "Très Urgent."

The next time Ursula went back with two scarves under her dress. Unfortunately the woman who wrote "Très Urgent" wasn't there, and another woman was at the counter. She told Ursula the 5th Bureau had no objection to her marriage. All she had to do now was have it signed by the 6th Bureau. She took the paper to the 6th Bureau, but there she was told no authorizations would be given out until Wednesday. The chief of the 6th Bureau was away.

Poor Ursula had only one more scarf left.

But it was nice to have her remain with me. Every boss hates to see a good secretary get married.

The Empire Black Dinner Dress Mystery

A STORY in *Figaro* informed me that the Paris dress designers have asked Interpol (The International Police) to aid them in stopping the pirating of their creations. Apparently there is a world-wide syndicate that steals the designs from the major dress houses and sells them to interested dress houses, stores, and manufacturers throughout the globe. Fortunes are lost through black-marketing of styles, and it's getting more serious all the time.

If Interpol accepts the assignment I can just imagine what will happen.

The phone rings in the Interpol headquarters in Paris, and Sergeant Vendredi answers it.

He says, "What? When? Where? How? Zut? Alors! Mais naturellement."

He hangs up and calls Inspector Boutique, of the Robe Voleur Bureau.

Inspector Boutique, roused out of a deep sleep, picks up the phone. His wife knows that it can mean only one thing, so slips into her Balenciaga cocktail dress and starts making a pot of coffee.

Sergeant Vendredi says on the phone, "Mon inspecteur, they have just stolen the Empire black-jet-beaded dinner dress from Dior."

"Not the one with the wide, crushed belt, the high-draped neckline and the narrow sheaths in the back?"

"Yes, that's the one. It had black satin ribbons and triangular points and a detachable cape."

"Mon Dieu, tell them not to touch anything. I'll be right down."

Inspector Boutique gets dressed hurriedly and drinks a cup of coffee.

"When will you be home?" his wife asks.

"I don't know. This may be a very tough case to crack. Don't wait up for me."

"I wish you would go back to the safe-cracking squad," his wife wails. "You haven't been home one night in the last three months."

"What can I do? It happens every year after the new collections."

He kisses her goodbye and speeds off to the Dior House on the Avenue Montaigne. There is a crowd in front of the house; the police have set up floodlights and the reporters are trying to get in.

Sergeant Vendredi is already there and he salutes the inspector.

"Upstairs on the first floor."

The reporters crowd around the inspector. "Is it the work of Lefty La Gauche?"

"I will have a statement in a half-hour, gentlemen. We

are already rounding up suspects, and there are several clues I don't wish to discuss."

He pushes through and goes up to the first floor. The body of a nude store mannequin is lying on the floor. Her plaster of Paris head has been broken off at the neck, and her arms are raised as if she had put up a struggle. The fingerprint men are just finishing up, and the police photographer has taken his final picture.

Inspector Boutique makes a few notes in his book. Vendredi is at his side. "Nothing has been touched. No screams were heard; the concierge didn't see anyone come in or go out. Yves Saint-Laurent is on vacation in the south of France. A black ribbon was found in the hall."

Inspector Boutique examines the body. "It's cold. The crime must have taken place early last night."

Vendredi says, "Do you think it could have been Lefty La Gouche?"

Inspector Boutique shakes his head. "Lefty La Gouche likes chiffon jersey sleeves. The sleeves on this model were puffy. Besides, he's in prison for the Balmain fingertip-length-jacket job.

"Let's talk to some of the employees," Inspector Boutique says.

They go into the salon where all the Dior employees are gathered. Many of them are crying. Inspector Boutique interrogates each one in turn. The head vendeuse says the dress was on the model when she left at six o'clock. Two assistant vendeuses confirm it.

"The Duchess of Windsor was going to buy it," the head vendeuse says tearfully. "Now it's gone and will probably appear in the Montgomery Ward catalog next week."

"It was our best model," the business manager confirms.

"Keep them here all morning," Boutique says to a detective.

"Where are we going?" Vendredi asks, once they're in the car.

"To Maxim's. I'll go in first. If I don't come out after two hours, come in and get me."

"You have a suspect?" Vendredi asks.

"No. I'm hungry."

Inspector Boutique goes into Maxim's, which is crowded with people. The headwaiter gives him a table behind a pole. Boutique orders a large dinner with a 1937 Dom Pérignon champagne. Suddenly he looks up on the dance floor. A man and a woman are dancing close together. He cuts in and takes the woman in his arms. "You're under arrest, Lefty La Droite, for the theft of the Dior Empire dinner dress."

"But you must be looking for my brother, Lefty La Gauche."

"I'm looking for you, Lefty La Droite. And you're wearing the dress, so I caught you with the goods on you."

He leads Lefty La Droite off the floor as people comment, "Isn't it a beautiful gown?"

"How did you know it was me?" Lefty La Droite asks, once they're in the police car.

The inspector takes a black bow out of his pocket.

"You were the only woman on the floor with a bow missing. Don't underestimate Interpol. We always get our man."

"I hope I get a sky gray mandarin jacket with a pajama cord in the center when I get to the Santé Prison," Lefty La Droite says hopefully.

Mme. Boutique is waiting in a new Givenchy draped-bosom, reversible suit. She is cleaning the house when the inspector walks in.

"What happened?" she asks, scrambling some eggs.

"Nothing," the inspector yawns. "It was a quiet night."

It's a Great Year for Wines

THE Grapevine had it that 1959 could well be one of the grandmothers of all wine years. As the grapes were being harvested, growers, vintners, brokers, imbibers, and bibers were heard to say to each other, "Mon Dieu, it may be as great as 1947, and surely it is not far behind '29." In order to see for myself, I took a train down to Bordeaux in the company of Alexis Lichine, a Russian-born, French-raised, naturalized American wine merchant and château owner. Mr. Lichine, who has been described as the Billy Graham of the wine business, has furthered the cause of French wines more than any single man in the United States. He has preached the gospel of the grape from the south of Carolina to the Top of the Mark, and has damned to hell all those who would have tea or coffee with their meals.

Mr. Lichine even talks about wine in his sleep. I know this for a fact because he fell asleep on the train going down to Bordeaux and I still talked to him.

It turns out there is a lot of ferment in the French wine business. The two major wine-producing areas in France are Bordeaux and Burgundy. Each proclaims its wine is the best and derides the value of the other. The Burgundians produce less wine, but are better at promoting it.

For one thing, Burgundy is located on the road to the Riviera and gets many more visitors than Bordeaux. For another, Nelson Eddy has managed for the last thirty years to keep the name alive in the public's mind every time he has sung "To Hell With Burgundy." Burgundy has also wisely taken everyone to its bosom through an organization called the Académie du Tastevin. Every so often in solemn ceremony the Burgundians don velvet robes and swear in new members of a world-wide fraternity. The Bordeaux people say you don't have to be an expert to be a member of the Tastevin. All you have to do is promise to push the stuff like mad.

One of the photos the Bordelais cherish—it appeared in a French newspaper—is that of a man being arrested for running a brothel. In the background of the photo is a diploma asserting that the man was a Chevalier in the Tastevin.

The Bordeaux people, on the other hand, are handicapped because they have four or five organizations who want no part of each other. The Sauternes won't mix with the Saint-Emilions, who are suspicious of the Médocs.

The Bordelais are only united when it comes to their thoughts on Burgundy.

For one thing, the Bordeaux wine people believe there is more monkey business going on in Burgundy than there is in Bordeaux, and most people in the business will agree. The Burgundians would like to think there is more monkey business going on in Bordeaux, but they can't prove it.

Also, the Bordeaux people have doctors on their side, who

think Bordeaux is better for you. On the other hand, if you order a Bordeaux in front of a Burgundian he'll ask if you're sick.

According to the Bordelais, anyone can drink Burgundy, but you have to be a connoisseur to appreciate Bordeaux wines.

Putting it in terms we can all understand, Burgundy is younger, more buxom, more forward, and promises a lot. It is a promiscuous wine. Bordeaux is more the intellectual type. It has the experience the Burgundies lack, and while it takes time to know, the rewards can be greater. "Every experienced lover," Mr. Lichine said in his sleep, "knows youth isn't everything."

It Puckers Your Mouth

"THERE are not in this world any lords of higher lineage than the great wines of Médoc, which form the first nobility of the vintages of France, whether they be Margaux, Saint-Julien, Saint-Estèphe, Paulliac, or Moulis. They rival each other in their incomparable elegance and in their rich, ruby-red color."

That is what they would have told you if you had gone to Bordeaux for the harvesting of the 1959 grapes. As a guest of Alexis Lichine, proprietor of the Château Prieuré-Lichine and Lascombes, I spent a few days in the Médoc, watching one of the great vintages being brought in. The sight was one to make the heart beat faster. The dry French summer and fall, which had played havoc with vegetables and dairy products, had been a boon to the grapes. Not only was it a great year in quality, but in quantity as well.

In one of those inexplicable French economic explanations we were told that the price of wine would not go down because it had been a successful year. The previous years, 1956, 1957, 1958, were bitter and cold years for the wine growers, and very little wine was made. The shortage sent the price up. This is reasonable. But last year, with wine in quantity, the price still went up.

I made the mistake of asking one of the growers why.

"Because," he said, as if talking to a child, "it is a great year and everybody wants it."

So much for the economics of wine.

M. Lichine promised to take me on a tour of the Médoc and we started, quite naturally, with his own Château Lascombes. He told me that in the course of the tour I would be asked to taste some wines and he didn't want me to disgrace him.

I practiced by tasting some wine from one of his vats. It tasted good, and I swallowed it.

"No, no, no," he said. "Don't swallow it. Swish it around in your mouth."

"Clockwise or counterclockwise?"

"Clockwise. Counterclockwise is for Burgundy. And then spit it on the floor."

I practiced a few times until I got it right.

"Now say something," he said.

"It sure puckers the inside of your mouth."

"No, that's not what you're supposed to say," M. Lichine cried. "You're supposed to say something beautiful like, "How full and generous. It will fulfill its promise."

"Okay, but it still puckers the inside of your mouth."

Our first stop was Château Margaux, one of the four greatest wine châteaux in France. We visited the chai, the long shed where the grapes are put in vats and barrels. The master of the chai asked me if I wanted to taste some. I nodded, and he gave me a glass.

I swished it around and spat it out. Lichine looked pleased at his pupil. "It has a texture all its own," I said, "It tastes like cotton."

Lichine kicked me in the leg. "What he means," he said to the master, "is that it tastes like velvet."

After we were shown around the Château (I discovered that no one in Bordeaux presses wine in their bare feet any more) Lichine took me to the Châteaux Latour, another of the four greatest vineyards in France.

I tasted the Latour wine and said, "A great wine. It has such a rich, soft flavor."

Lichine smiled.

"Could I have some water?" I asked of the owner, Count Hubert de Beaumont.

Lichine's face dropped.

"Water?" The count looked puzzled. "Do you want to wash your hands?"

Before I could say I wanted to drink the water, Lichine dragged me away.

"Never, never, never ask for water in Bordeaux," he admonished me.

"But I tell you my mouth is all puckered up. My cheeks are stuck to my teeth."

Lichine would have none of it. The last château we visited belonged to Philippe de Rothschild, owner of the

Mouton-Rothschild vineyards. M. Rothschild, a gracious host, showed us through his caves and invited us to have a glass of champagne with him in his house, one of the most beautiful in France.

We went upstairs and a servant served us each a bubbling glass. Lichine toasted his host and we each sipped some. Then as Lichine looked on in horror, I swished it around in my mouth.

He screamed, "No!"

But it was too late. I spat it on the floor.

Two Poets in Paris

THE so-called beat generation of the United States hadn't made too much of a mark on Paris. But thanks to two American poets, Allen Ginsberg and Gregory Corso, things are looking up. Mr. Ginsberg, who went to Columbia University, and Mr. Corso, who came out of Dannemora Prison, were traveling around Europe reading their poems and preaching the gospel of the new American poetry.

"We've changed the course of poetry in the United States," said Mr. Ginsberg. "Do you realize what that means? There's been a revolution in poetry, and we've done it. There is no equivalent to it in France. England is dead. They're in the cellar with Gambic."

"Dame Edith Sitwell," said Mr. Corso, "told us the hope of English poetry is in America. She also gave us tea and water-cress sandwiches."

Mr. Ginsberg tried to explain exactly what the beat generation had done for poetry. "We're experimenting; we have a new basis of measure. We measure our lines by breath, not by beat. Give us time and we'll take over from the priests. We have a message. People have to understand. Our mission is to make them."

"The square poets," said Mr. Corso, "don't dig what we're doing. Their horror is they take their form from Auden's first page 'In Breughel's Icares' for instance . . . and Marianne Moore's 'Durer would have liked living in this town.' None of their poems start with 'Fried Shoes.' Our poetry is Whambam, whatever comes to our mind. That's our message."

Mr. Corso, who has a book of poems called "Gasoline," was twenty-eight years old. He spent three years in Dannemora for robbery and got out when he was twenty years old. Unlike many men who leave prison, Mr. Corso said he found love and beauty in prison, and the books he read in prison made him decide to be a poet.

As a poet, he said, he's taken a vow of poverty, but he added, "It's hard to live up to it because I like Lucifer too much."

"How do you get by?" I asked.

"It isn't easy," said Mr. Corso. "None of the foundations will give us any money. They don't dig us. I get money from girls. Every time I meet a girl I ask her how much money she has, and then I demand half of it. I'm not doing anything wrong with money. I just use it to buy food."

Things hadn't been too easy for the two poets, even when they had an opportunity to read their poetry. In Paris they held a reading in the Mistral, a Left Bank bookshop. There were forty or fifty people in attendance.

"Unfortunately," said Mr. Ginsberg, "another poet was reciting some uncommunicative junk and we didn't like it."

"I protested it wasn't real poetry," Mr. Corso said. "Someone asked me what I meant by real poetry. So I took off all my clothes and read my poems naked."

"Did they get the message?"

"I had two big, bearded friends of mine as bodyguards and they threatened they'd beat up anybody who left while I was reciting. I was a big success."

"It was a mild reading," said Mr. Ginsberg, "compared to some I've been to in San Francisco.

Both poets were invited to read at Oxford to a group of about one hundred students. For the occasion Mr. Corso wrote a poem in praise of the atom bomb.

Oxford students have been protesting against the atom and hydrogen bombs, and Mr. Corso's poem didn't go over too well.

Part of it went:

"BOOM all ye skies and BOOM all ye suns BOOM ye
moons
"and ye stars BOOM and ye nights BOOM;
"BOOM ye days and BOOM ye winds, ye clouds,
ye rains, BOOM BOOM
"BANGBOOM ye lakes BING
"BANGBOOM ye rivers BING
"BANGBONGBOOM ye forests;
"Yes! yes! when the first bomb died
"flowers lept in joy their roots aching!

"Fields knelt proud beneath the halleluyahs of the wind!
"Pink bombs blossomed! Elkbombs perked their ears!
"Ah many a bomb that day did awe the bird a gentle
look——"

At about this point someone in the audience threw a shoe at Mr. Corso.

"It wasn't even a good English shoe," Mr. Corso complained.

"Some idiot asked me, after I read the poem, how would I like to die by a bomb. He missed the whole point. What I was saying is that you should rise above the bomb. You shouldn't hate it; you should love it. Intelligent people are the only ones who can love. If people love, they won't destroy. They didn't dig it. We called them all creeps and left. Only the girls followed us out to talk to us."

Even Pablo Picasso didn't dig Mr. Corso. Mr. Corso met the master in the south of France. "I got a thing about brown. Brown to me is biscuits which taste like sardines to the tongue of God. I asked what Picasso thought of brown and he thought I was talking about the color. When I told him what I really meant he hit me over the head with his hat. He shouldn't have hit me."

"What did you tell him?"

"I said, 'All love to poetry, and nuts to painters.'"

The poets have voracious appetites.

When Mr. Ginsberg met Marcel Duchamps, the French painter, he said, "I ate his shoe."

At the same party Mr. Corso was talking with Man Ray, the photographer and painter.

"Man Ray was eating a green cookie," said Mr. Corso,

"and I asked him why he didn't eat the white ones. He said he only ate things the color of his tie. So I ate his tie."

"Why?"

"To show him I dug him. But I got sick."

Both poets felt they'd given all they could to Paris. Mr. Ginsberg wanted to go back to America if he could raise the fare, and Mr. Corso wanted to go to India.

Paris will never be the same without them.

A Matter of Pride

PARIS is supposed to be a city of romance, but I wasn't quite sure why until I talked to three young girls who have lived in Paris for a few years. The girls, all foreigners, were comparing notes on Frenchmen, and it got so interesting I received permission to take a few notes of my own.

"Young Frenchmen," said one of the young ladies, "all have the same line. Suppose you are sitting alone at a sidewalk café, and a Frenchman sees you reading a foreign newspaper or book. First he will kick you in the heel or bump you 'accidentally.'

"Then he will say in French, 'Excuse me, Mademoiselle. I am so sorry. I hope I did not hurt you.' Then he looks under the table at your leg, not so much to see what damage he has done, but to see whether it's worth going on.

"If he thinks so, he says, 'I see you are a foreigner. What is your nationality?'

"If you say you are an American he says, 'Oh, America,

I love America. I had a cousin who once visited Montreal and brought me back a present.'

"You say nothing.

" 'How long have you been here?' he asks. 'Your French is excellent.' He says this even if you don't speak a word.

"If you reply, 'Six months or a year,' he brightens up. 'Then you must know Paris and the French very well.' The implication is 'Then you must know how we do things over here.'

" 'How long are you staying?' This is a very important question. If you say five years, he wants to forget the whole thing for fear of complications. If you say only a few months, he becomes tearful and sentimental. 'Oh, you're leaving so soon? How sad for me.'

"Then he wants to know what you're doing here. If you say you're a student, then you have a high priority. French boys feel that foreign girl students who can afford to study in France usually come from well-to-do families.

"The French boys also keep alive the legend that a foreign girl in Paris is bound to do things she wouldn't do at home.

"If you say you're a tourist, you get a low priority. A Frenchman considers a tourist an expensive item. And before there is a chance for a romance he has to take her to the Eiffel Tower, the Louvre, Notre Dame Cathedral, the Bateaux Mouches, Sacré Coeur, and the wax museum. By the time the tour is over, and just when the Frenchman, having invested his time and money, is about to make his move, a uniformed guide from Thomas Cook shows up at her hotel and whisks her off for the train to Venice."

"What happens if you say you are a student?" I asked.

"Then the Frenchman beams all over and says, 'Do you

know Victor Hugo.' If you admit you do, he behaves as if you've both got a friend in common, and there is no reason for you to be strangers.

"When the preliminary questions are over the serious part of the interview takes place. 'Where do you live?' If you reply, 'With a French family,' his face falls. If you say, 'In the dormitory at the Cité Universitaire,' he also becomes depressed. But if you say, 'In a hotel in Montparnasse,' he smiles, takes your hand in his, and says, 'May I buy you a drink?' "

One of the other girls added, "The approach just described is usually made by students and young Frenchmen. An older Frenchman who can afford to ask you to dinner presents far more problems. A Frenchman will never ask you to have dinner with him. He'll ask you to spend an agreeable evening with him. Dinner, in his opinion, is only the first part of it. Although the French are supposed to be great gourmets, when they take a new girl out for dinner food is the farthest thing from their minds.

"During the meal they are constantly selling themselves, and the success they have with women.

"From there on the discussion goes on to where you will go after dinner. The only place he wants to go is to his apartment. If you say No, he gets very hurt and angry and says, 'But I thought it was agreed upon.' The discussion will continue at a sidewalk café until two in the morning. A Frenchman is willing to plead his case all night if you let him. If you still say No, he may become rude. If you're an American girl, he says, 'It's about time you American girls woke up.' If you are a Scandinavian girl, he will say, 'Then it's true, Scandinavian girls are as cold as stone.' If you're a German girl, he'll say, 'All you can think about is Germany,' and if you're a French girl he'll say, 'I know. You're saving your love for an American.' "

The third girl at the table said a Frenchman will never take a girl out more than three times unless he falls in love with her.

"He usually gives up after the first time, unless a friend he has met on the previous evening calls him the next day and says, 'Would you introduce me to that lovely girl you were with last night?' If this happens, he decides perhaps it's worth a second try. Only in rare cases will a rebuffed suitor go for the third time, and this time only for black coffee at a dingy sidewalk café."

"The most interesting thing about Frenchmen," the first girl said, "is if something happens between him and you, he pretends on your next meeting that nothing happened at all. But if nothing happened he pretends in front of his friends that everything happened. I guess it's a question of pride."

SOME DAYS LATER A FRENCHMAN STRIKES BACK

Dear Sir:

I was horrified to read in your paper about your conversation with three foreign girls who were discussing the attitudes of Frenchmen toward women. I think it is only fair to demand equal time to present our side of the picture. Otherwise this slander will be taken as fact and may make many attractive young ladies cancel their trips to our wonderful country.

It is true that the Frenchman consider himself an expert in the art of wooing a woman. But very few women I have come in contact with have complained about the treatment they have been accorded in Paris by Frenchmen, and if anything, we have sent women back to all parts of the world happier, wiser, and more contented than they ever were before.

Foreign women are naturally attracted to Frenchmen, because Frenchmen are naturally attracted to women. From a very early age we are taught that a woman is the most wonderful thing in the world, and a Frenchman's role is to please her in every way he can.

Anglo-Saxon and American women, who are not used to being treated as women, are suspicious of the attentions they receive from Frenchmen, but once they get over these suspicions they realize they have found a race of men who are passionately devoted to them, and are willing to devote their lives, even their money, to fulfilling every woman's dreams.

The description of a Frenchman trying to pick up a foreign girl in a sidewalk café could only have been described by an American girl. The Frenchmen behave in this manner only because it is expected of them.

A Frenchman would much rather say to a girl he is attracted to, "You are beautiful and I am in love with you and would you have a drink with me?"

But this approach would only frighten the young thing, and she might start screaming for the police. Therefore we are obligated to go through the boring formalities, not because we want to, but because the American way of life (and the English) demands it.

The Frenchman is penalized, not for the way he behaves, but for the way other nationalities behave toward their women. An American and an English girl (they are the outstanding examples) are taught at a very early age never to talk to strangers, and it's good advice in their own countries, where men treat women with brutality and disrespect.

But in Latin countries a man is not being disrespectful when he talks to a strange girl. He is saying what is in his heart at the moment, and he is saying what he believes a woman wants to hear.

What the foreign girl does not understand is that a Frenchman is not discouraged by defeat as much as he pretends to be. His whole life has been one defeat after another, and if he brags about his triumphs it is only because they are so few and bring back such pleasant memories.

It is true that a Frenchman will discuss the problem with the young lady as long as she is willing to stay up, but he depends only on his verbal powers of persuasion and even if the evening comes to naught, he considers it a wonderful intellectual exercise.

The world owes a great debt to Frenchmen. If it weren't for Frenchmen there wouldn't be French perfumes, beautiful French clothes, and beautiful French women. French women will do anything to be attractive because they know Frenchmen care.

We Frenchmen have our faults, but not knowing how to treat women is not one of them. And I'm not talking about Brigitte Bardot.

Sincerely,
Count Artois de Buchwald.

How Fashions Are Made

THE new fashion collections are on again in Paris, and the town is once again loaded with fashion reporters, manufacturers, department store buyers, accessory experts, and style thieves, all of whom are interested in seeing what the French couturiers have up their sleeves for this summer.

The trend is to get fashions back to normal, and for the moment all wild body styles have gone out of fashion. Very few people are aware of how fashion ideas are created, and it was just by chance that I happened to stagger in on a secret meeting of one of the biggest fashion houses and witness the birth of next summer's collection.

At the meeting were the production manager, the head vendeuse, the publicity director, and the treasurer, all sitting around a table. There was an empty chair at the head of the table, presumably reserved for The Man, or, as he is known in France, Le Maître.

Suddenly the door opened and a sixteen-year-old boy, chewing on a piece of licorice, was led into the room by his mother. Everyone in the room stood up and bowed.

The mother placed the boy in the chair, straightened his tie, and stood by his arm, staring coldly at the group.

The production manager spoke first, "Well, Maître, have you made your decision?"

The Maître smiled, but didn't say anything.

The head vendeuse said, "Are you going to put the hips on the bosom this year?"

The Maître shook his head.

"Perhaps," said the publicity director, "you will put the waist around the knees?"

The Maître shook his head again.

"The bosom around the hips?" the treasurer suggested.

The Maître sucked his licorice stick, but said nothing.

The production manager said, "I know. You're going to put the bosom on the back and the back on the shoulders. you will call it the Backward Look."

"No, no, no," the Maître said.

The people at the table looked gloomy. "Perhaps," the treasurer said, "you are going to lower the bosom and raise the skirt."

Silence.

"You're not going to lower the skirt and raise the bosom?" the publicity director asked incredulously.

"You're all in a rut," the Maître said. "We want new ideas, but all the time it's the same thing, the same suggestions, the same ideas. The customers want something fresh, something new, something they've never had before."

"What is that, Maître?" the production manager said. "Tell us. You are our leader."

"I am going to do something revolutionary, something we will be criticized for, something which will shake the very foundations of the industry."

"Oh, tell us, Maître," quivered the head vendeuse.

The Maître took the licorice stick out of his mouth and pointed it at the group. "I am going to put the waist where the waist belongs."

There was a shocked silence and then the publicity director screamed, "Maître, you've done it again."

"And I'm going to put the bosom on the bosom."

"Mother of pearl!" whistled the production manager.

"And the hips will be on the hips," the Maître said, slamming his tiny fist on the table.

"And skirts?" asked the treasurer. "What will you do about skirts?"

The Maître stared at them and he announced dramatically, "Skirts will be normal length."

"No one's ever thought of it before," the head vendeuse cried. "Oh, Maître, you are a genius."

Suddenly the production manager stood up. "It's all well and good, Maître, and I hate to pour cold water on this meeting, but if you start making dresses that look like dresses, the husbands are going to like it."

"He's right," admitted the treasurer. "If the husbands like the clothes, we'll be ruined. No women will buy them."

The Maître scowled. "It's only for one season. Next season we'll do something different. Making normal clothes is a fad. The shock effect will sell the clothes. By the time the shock wears off, we'll have the bosom back at the knees where it belongs."

"It's true," the publicity director said. "The effect will be so startling the husbands won't have time to recover."

The Maître picked up his licorice stick. "Then it's decided. We shall call the line 'The Natural Look.' "

Everyone said it together, "The Natural Look."

The head vendeuse wept unashamedly. "Oh, creator, what could we do without you?"

The treasurer kissed his hand.

"Thank heaven you're not old enough to be drafted."

The mother spoke up for the first time. "My son has to take his nap."

Everyone stood up, and the Maître took his mother's hand and left the room.

The Secret of Dieting

THE most discouraging thing about living in Paris is the amount of weight one seems to gain during the course of a three-hundred-sixty-five-day year. The two-hour lunch, the three-hour dinner, and the occasional onion soup after the theater weigh heavily on most of us.

If it wasn't for my friends from the United States, who are constantly filling me with such frightening words as cholesterol, obesity, ectomorph, metabolism, and Gayelord Hauser, I wouldn't give it a second thought. But Americans are diet mad and at the moment, next to the Russians, there is nothing they fear more than overweight.

Last summer, I decided to go on a crash diet which friends said was guaranteed to make me lose twenty pounds in a month. It consisted of coffee or tea in the morning and nothing else. For lunch, grilled meat, no salt; seven ounces of green vegetables, no salt; two ounces of Gruyère cheese or one ounce of yogurt, a choice of an orange or an apple. The same went for dinner. I wasn't allowed to drink anything with meals, and I was only allowed a pint of water a day.

Since diet comes from the verb to die, I was thinking

seriously of committing suicide instead. But I would only give solace to the insurance companies, who insist overweight people have a shorter span of life.

The first day was fine. Although I fainted twice, I managed to get through the day by going to bed at eight.

The next morning my wife insisted an egg with breakfast wouldn't hurt me, and since she is wiser than I am in these matters (she only weighs one hundred nineteen pounds), I assumed she knew what she was talking about.

At noon I lunched with a friend who told me I was only kidding myself. "Meat is more fattening than potatoes," he said. "My doctor lets me eat all the potatoes I want to, without butter, of course." I have always respected this friend's judgment (he's made a million dollars in the stock market), and so I had potatoes with my meat.

In the evening I dined at the home of a French wine dealer. He was shocked to think I wouldn't drink with my dinner. He pointed out that wine was the best digestif in the world and unless I digested my food I would gain weight automatically. It made sense, and I had a half-bottle of a very extraordinary and honest Burgundy.

The next day things went a little better. An American visitor said one teaspoon of cream was three times as fattening as one teaspoon of sugar, so I had sugar in my coffee instead of cream.

Another friend said doing without salt at meals was foolish because it only reduced the water in my body, which wasn't fat and which would automatically come back as soon as I went off the crash diet.

A third friend told me that the best way to lose weight was to eat nothing but starches. This man's brother-in-law lost ten pounds that way, he said. I've always been fond of spaghetti, and I had a bowl for my lunch just to see if his brother-in-law knew what he was talking about.

In the evening my wife reported her hairdresser said fresh lobster or shrimp or crab meat were nonfattening, and since she couldn't remember which one I liked, she bought all three. I couldn't remember either, so I ate all of them.

The fourth day is always the hardest when you're on a crash diet, I was told. If you can get by it, the rest of the month is easy. I got by it by having scrambled eggs and toast for breakfast, chicken à la king for lunch, and a cheese soufflé for dinner. It wasn't as hard to get by as everyone says. It's all in the mind.

I'm still continuing the crash program, but I've lined up an entirely new set of people to eat with. Each one has his own ideas about dieting, and I'm willing to listen to everybody. The main thing about going on a diet is not to go it alone. You need friends to give you encouragement, and if it wasn't for the people I've talked to already, I don't think I would ever make it.

The Frenchman and His Car

NOT long ago a man was arrested in the Bois de Boulogne, Paris' largest park, for *misbehaving* with a woman (not his wife) in a tiny Renault automobile. The man pleaded not guilty on the grounds that it was physically impossible to misbehave in a Renault 4 CV. The judge who had never tried it, turned the question over to several experts who came back in a few weeks with the following verdict: It was difficult to misbehave in a Renault 4 CV, but not impossible. The man was found guilty.

The reason the trial attracted so much attention in France was not that it concerned *misbehavior*, since the French don't even recognize such a thing, nor that the woman in question was another man's wife, but that an automobile was involved. The average Frenchman loves his automobile, and the only reason he wouldn't misbehave in it is he is afraid to damage his car.

There is probably nothing as dear to a Frenchman as his automobile. He may take his wife for granted, but his car is something he lavishes love and affection on and keeps on a pedestal when he isn't trying to get through traffic.

If you so much as bump his bumper, the Frenchman will jump out of his car, raging mad, and scream for a half-hour about the crime you have committed against his prized possession. But if you knock over his wife in a department store, he will shrug his shoulders and may even apologize for his wife's getting in your way.

It is safe to say that if a Frenchman has the choice between a car and a woman, he will in almost all cases take the car. For one thing a Frenchman has only one car, but he usually has access to many women.

Unlike Americans, the French do not consider their automobiles status symbols. The French divide themselves between those who have cars and those who don't. The man who drives a small Simca, a Peugeot, or Renault has no inferiority complex toward someone who drives a large

Citroen, Versailles, or Mercedes-Benz. As a matter of fact, if anything, the driver of the smaller car is more aggressive about it and, like small people, feels protected because of size.

This doesn't always work. Once I was standing at the Place de la Concorde when a four-door Buick bumped a Simca Aronde. The driver of the Simca got out of his car red-faced and started to scream at the Buick owner, also a Frenchman.

"You are an imbecile and an idiot," the Simca owner screamed. "Look what you have done to my bumper. You scratched it. You should be thrown into prison and your horrible car with you."

The Buick owner stood by passively as the Simca owner went on and on shouting epithets and threats. I thought the Buick owner was going to hit the other man. But instead he got back into the Buick, backed it up about ten feet, stepped on the gas, and smashed into the back of the Simca crushing it like an accordion.

Then the Buick owner got out of his car and said to the Simca man who was speechless, "There, now you have something to scream about."

It is hard to describe the passion a Frenchman has for his car. For one thing, it is rare that an eighteen- or nineteen-year-old French boy owns an automobile. For another, his father would never let him use the family car. So most Frenchmen must wait a long time before they possess a motor vehicle, much longer than they have to wait to possess a French girl. Therefore, while most of them have experienced a woman at an early age, few of them have experienced the pleasure of sitting behind the wheel of a car. Since a Frenchman has to work harder and longer for an automobile, it is only natural he would love it more.

Once the Frenchman has his car he treats it like a jealous lover. He feels, and rightly so, his car is the only one on the road, and he becomes frantic if anyone else comes near it. Although a Frenchman is considered an expert when it comes to making love, all Frenchmen are amateurs when it comes to driving a car. There is only one rule that they obey—that is, the car coming from the right has the right of the way. After that it's every man for himself.

In August 1954 the Paris Prefect (Chief of Police) decided to stop all horn-honking in Paris. This came as a blow to the French driver—for many drivers the horn on a car was the most attractive part of the body, and there was nothing that gave a Frenchman more pleasure than pressing down on it at every corner.

Strangely enough, the Chief of Police's edict worked, and ever since then there has been no horn-blowing in Paris. Now there is only shouting and arms flailing away on the sides of automobile doors.

If the French driver gives short shrift to other cars, he has no shrift for pedestrians. The late Fred Allen was once wondering why there are so many churches in Paris. Then he discovered that it was because it gave someone an opportunity to stop in and pray before crossing a street.

It is very hard for a foreigner who is unfamiliar with French drivers to catch on to driving in Paris.

A few simple things to keep in mind might help them.

1. If someone extends his hand, that means the window is open.

2. If someone stops at a red light, it means his foot has slipped off the accelerator.

3. If the left rear blinker light is lit, it means the car will either turn left, right, or come at you in reverse.

4. If the right rear blinker light is lit, it means the car ahead will either stop or has a short circuit.

5. If you hear curses coming from another car, it means that you have done something that irks the other driver because he didn't think of it first.

6. Sounding the horn means the car has just struck a pedestrian and the driver would like someone to be a witness.

7. A policeman with one hand up means he has just witnessed a very gory accident and doesn't have the nerve to look at it. He is shielding his eyes with the other hand.

8. When a driver waves his hand up and down it means the girl with him is not his wife, and he would appreciate all courtesies.

Survival in August

AS EVERYONE knows, August is the month when every Frenchman in Paris goes on vacation. On July 31, all the storekeepers slam down their iron shutters; electricians, plumbers, and garage men pack in their tools; and factories, offices, stores, government buildings, restaurants, and dry-cleaning establishments shut down for the entire month.

In previous years, when the Parisians returned in September, they found the skeletons of many foreigners in positions indicating they had been trying to get into a closed bakery, a drugstore, or a laundry.

Among the more tragic cases was one of a man who was found in front of a restaurant, clutching his half-eaten Diners' Club credit card in one hand. The body was still warm and indicated the man had expired only twenty-four hours before the restaurant reopened for the autumn season.

Another was of a woman who was found floating underneath the ceiling of her apartment. Next to her was a piece of paper with the number of a plumber on it. Apparently the woman had been trying all month to get the plumber, and finally the water got too high for her to reach the phone. The police said phoning wouldn't have done her any good as the plumber was in Brittany.

Still another case was that of a tourist whose car broke down at the Place de la Concorde. Instead of leaving the car to seek out help, he remained behind the wheel, waiting for someone from the Automobile Club to tow him away. Naturally, no one came; and finally, without water, he perished, not realizing he was only a few yards from the Seine.

Another tourist became so desperate because all the laundries were closed that he broke into a locked Bendix laundromat and tried to wash his own shirt. He was caught and is now doing twenty years at the Santé Prison.

And who will ever forget the day in August 1955 when four people were killed and thirty-six injured on the Champs Elysées fighting over a lone taxicab which had come in from Deauville by mistake?

Every year the situation has become grimmer, but this year a group of foreigners who have to remain in Paris to take care of visiting firemen have decided to do something about it.

The first idea was to appeal to the International Red Cross in Geneva, but the appeal met with no success, because the International Red Cross turned it over to the French Red Cross, and everyone at the French Red Cross was going on vacation.

So the group of foreigners decided to form a nonprofit organization called the Society of People Stuck in Paris in August or, as it will soon be known, SOPSIPIA.

SOPSIPIA, in its first meeting decided to issue survival kits at cost. The survival kits for men include a Dacron shirt, a Wash 'n' Dri suit, a role of film, a bottle of Brut champagne, a croissant, three haricots verts, a copy of *Lady Chatterley's Lover*, and a Do-It-Yourself Strip Tease Act.

The women's survival kit includes a box of Kleenex, a box of Tide, a set of post cards, a brioche, a home permanent, a green salad, another box of Kleenex, and a glass string bag for window shopping.

At its first meeting, the committee also decided to set up free Vichyssoise kitchens in front of Thomas Cook and the American Express.

Courses in survival will be given at Maxim's and the Tour d'Argent, and a place on the banks of the Seine will be set aside for wives who wish to do laundry.

Many American companies are co-operating with SOPSIPIA. Pan American Airways is running a contest in Paris, in which the winner of the first prize will receive an American plumber for a week-end.

TWA is also running a contest. The winner of its contest will have his suit flown to New York for dry cleaning.

These and many more things make for one of the most exciting August Paris has seen in years. I only wish I could be here to see it. But unfortunately I'm going on vacation.

6. "The Seven Deadly Arts"

The Health Nuts

"HOLLYWOOD is on a new kick," said Larry Gelbart, a TV writer who was filling me in on the latest American fads. "First it was psychiatry, then it was dieting, and now the health nuts have taken over. Many of those motion-picture stars and comedians, having done everything to their heads and the outside of their bodies, are now turning inward to help themselves. As part of the campaign for self-improvement, they have become organic food specialists. Instead of food, they're eating dandelion hearts, roots of moss, and eucalyptus bark. It's very dangerous to be invited to someone's house for a meal. For one thing, you can't walk on their lawn because that may be your dinner. For another, it isn't enough that your friends are health nuts; they spend the whole evening trying to convert everyone else.

"I was invited to the house of a Hollywood couple a month ago. They had a little girl, aged five. Unfortunately I had a cold and I was sniffling.

"The father turned to the little girl and said, 'You see what happened to Uncle Larry because he ate lamb chops.'

"It's hard to get a drink in a health nut's house. They either offer you a glass of honey or a handful of sunflower seeds. I was trying to think of some reason why I couldn't stay for dinner, but it was too late. The butler announced dinner was served. Dinner? It consisted of boiled peanut water, wheat-germ pancakes, soya beans cooked in their own soy, carrot salad, and cider vinegar. But this wasn't all. After we ate the food the butler came in wiith a silver tray filled with jars of pills.

" 'What are these for?' I asked foolishly.

" 'They're the supplements,' the hostess explained.

" 'The supplements for what?'

"They thought I was crazy. 'For the things we didn't eat,' she said. 'The brown bottle is a bread supplement; the green bottle is the salt supplement; the red bottle is the protein supplement; the black bottle is the starch supplement; the red-white-and-blue bottle is the vitamin supplement; and the tall bottle with the clear liquid is the energy tonic.'

"I said I was full and I just couldn't eat any more, but the hostess seemed very upset. She said the druggist had been preparing the meal all day, and he would be very hurt if I didn't eat everything.

"After dinner we went into the living room to hear the little girl play the piano. She played very well, and her father said, 'That was very good, dear. You can now have a piece of candy.' And, so help me, he went to a bin, and handed her a raw potato.

"After this experience, I started to look into the health craze in Hollywood. It seems now if you have a small party, you hire the family doctor. But if it's more than twenty people it's catered by the Mayo Clinic.

"The reason this thing is spreading so fast is that there are usually about thirty people dependent on one star for their living. So in order to keep their jobs they have to go on health kicks too. The same men who used to sit around Schwabs Drug Store eating cheesecake and laughing at their boss's jokes are now eating weed sandwiches at the Cavendish Health Bar — and they're not laughing quite as loud.

"One of the big things for the health nuts is tiger's milk. I made the mistake one night of asking a comedian who drinks it four times a day, 'How do you milk a tiger?' I suggested, perhaps you have to sit on a short stool with a long gun, and do it very gently. But he didn't think it was very funny and I didn't get the job.

"The health addicts don't laugh much, and I can understand why. They figure they'll be around for a hundred and fifty years, and you've got, at the most (if you keep eating steak and apple pie), four years. So they feel, How can they laugh at another man who is just about to die?

"The only thing worse than going to a health addict's house for dinner is his coming to yours. He arrives with his little plastic bag of super-nutritional cereal, tiger's milk, and tea herbs, and says to your wife, 'Just give me a bottle of hot water.' Then, while the rest of the guests sit transfixed, their turkey getting cold, he starts mixing it all into a soup plate, tastes it, smacks his lips and says, 'I just signed a contract to do a film for M-G-M in A.D. 2960.'

"It's kind of tough on the kids. They don't really understand about health foods, and I know one kid who used to hide advertisements for cake mixes under his mattresses. His mother caught him and had his father give the kid a licking for keeping dirty pictures."

Someone's in a Fixing With Dinah

It's confession time for all television people, and, before anyone finds out about it, I think I'd better tell all. I was in a fixed Dinah Shore television show. The whole thing was rehearsed from beginning to end, and I was told what to say before I went on the air.

This is what happened. There had been so much scandal involved with television that the producers of Miss Shore's show decided they had to go abroad to find people who weren't implicated in one way or another — either because they had appeared on a TV quiz show, or because they had watched one.

A certain Mr. Bob Finkel, the producer of the show, came to Paris last summer and asked me to come on the show.

"There's three thousand bucks in it for you," he said, "if you say the right things on the program."

"But," I protested, "I don't know what to say to Dinah Shore on television. I'd make a muck of it."

Finkel patted me on the arm. "Don't worry, kid, we'll tell you what to say. We have preliminary rehearsals. Dinah will ask you questions, and all you have to do is sweat a little and answer them."

"What kind of questions?"

Finkel said, "Well, this is a show about Paris. You're going to be a device so we can go through Paris with

Dinah. Suppose she asked you who is the greatest singer in France, who would you say?"

"Yves Montand?"

"Nope, you're wrong. Montand isn't going to be on that week. You have to say Eddie Constantine. But don't just blurt it out. Think about it for a minute."

"Eddie Constantine."

"That's good. Okay, now suppose she said she wanted to go to the theater. What theater?"

"The Folies-Bergère?"

"You're wrong again. We've got Marcel Marceau, the pantomime artist, booked. You tell her to go to the Ambigu Theater to see Marcel Marceau. Let me try one more on you. Dinah says, 'Art, where is the greatest cancan in the world?'

I pursed my lips, held my head, wiped my brow. "At Twentieth Century-Fox Studios?"

"No," Finkel said with impatience, "the answer is the Moulin Rouge."

I protested I could never do it. Somebody would find out about it, and I'd be ruined. But Finkel said they could break his legs, and he'd never tell I had been given the answers in advance.

"I tell you what we'll do. You play along with us and we'll bring your wife to Hollywood also," he said.

"That doesn't sound like much fun to me," I said.

"Shut up!" he said. "You're in this too deep now to get out of it. I've got a good show and you're not going to ruin it."

I had no alternative but to accept. For a week Finkel rehearsed me every day with Miss Shore. As far as I know,

Miss Shore had no idea the show was rigged. She thought the answers I gave her were legitimate ones.

As I neared show time, I started to have my doubts. Forty million Americans believed in me. But there was the three thousand dollars, and my wife had already spent it on clothes for the children. I had to go on.

To make it easier on me, Finkel had cue cards made up with the answers to the questions. When Miss Shore asked me where she should go at night I wanted to say the Lido night club. But instead I had to say the Paris Opera because the ballet dancers Liane Daydé and Michel Renault were on the show. When she asked me what she should do in the daytime, I had to say the Louvre. I wanted to lose and bow out, but Finkel wouldn't let me.

Finally, just before it was all over, I muffed the last question. Dinah was supposed to ask me how she should fly back and I was suppossed to say, "Via Pan American." Instead I said, "By Marcel Marceau." But the program was over by then, and no one seemed to care.

In my original statement to the grand jury I said I wasn't given the answers. But it's not true.

If I had it to do all over again, I would have left my wife at home and spent the three thousand dollars on myself.

The Seville Feria

As MY jazz musician friends might put it, I did the Seville-ville bit. That is to say I went to the grandmother of all Spanish ferias, the famed Seville festival, where a man could lose his head or, at the very least, a finger to some lovely senorita's castanets.

The two greatest ferias of Spain are held in Pamplona in July and Seville in April. The Pamplona feria is a man's festival, featuring Spanish men running through the streets of the town followed by ferocious fighting bulls. The Seville feria is a woman's festival, featuring Spanish men running through streets followed by beautiful women on horseback. It goes on for five days and five nights, and a man can run out of breath by the fourth day if he isn't careful.

The Seville feria started in 1847 (a great year for ferias) as a cattle fair. The Andalusian farmers and landowners brought in their cattle, donkeys, and horses to sell to each other. Then one day one of the cattlemen put up a tent to shade his family from the sun.

The wife of another cattle dealer said to her husband, "You call yourself a seller of cows. Look at what Don Salamander has done for his she-donkey while I must perspire in the sun." (The dialogue loses something in the translation.)

"Woman, I am only human."

But his wife said, "You are a piebald ox. I want a tent, too."

So the cattle dealer, who was only human, set up a tent and also put in a table.

Another wife had words with her husband, and so he put up a tent with a table and chairs. Still another put up one with a table and chairs *and* a vase of flowers on the table.

And so it went until the fairgrounds were crowded with tents, and the women were trying to outdo each other.

As the years went by, the tents were replaced by one- and two-room wooden houses called casetas, and pretty soon they were so numerous there was little place left to sell the cattle. As a matter of fact, most of the Andalusians were so busy building and decorating their casetas they forgot all about the cattle. Until today the cattle are sold in another part of town, and the fair has become a great social event in which the only things traded are the daughters of the landowners.

As anyone who has been to Spain knows, the unmarried daughters of Spain are kept locked behind iron grillwork for a good portion of the year. It is only at the feria that they are brought out to be displayed by their proud parents. The women get dressed up in their flamenco costumes and gypsy dresses and ride sidesaddle through the streets of the feria. Some sit behind their fathers, others behind their brothers, and in the case of the Americans stationed near by, behind their commanding officers. The parade starts at noon and goes on until two thirty in the afternoon, when everyone goes into a caseta to have a bottle of amontillado and an olive.

In the meantime, the children of Seville, all dressed in costume, start their flamenco dancing, which they continue until *only* four in the morning because they have to go to school the next day.

Lunch is at four, and then everybody goes to the inevitable bullfight at five thirty. At eight people go home for the afternoon siesta, cocktails at the Alfonso XIII start at ten thirty, and everyone has an early dinner at midnight so he can get back to the fairgrounds for the all-night action.

"The feria," a Spanish Francophile told me, "is the only

time a man can talk to a woman he does not know, and she will talk back. The high mix with the low, and it is a beautiful thing to see."

"What does one say to a woman?" I asked him.

"You must compliment her. That is the only thing a Spanish woman wants to hear."

"How does one do that?"

"Say whatever is in your heart."

"Like what?"

"For example. Here is a mother walking with her beautiful daughter. I will show you."

He rattled off some Spanish to the pair. The daughter blushed, and the mother smiled and thanked him.

"What did you say?"

"I said, I cannot believe that from one little church you could produce a cathedral like this daughter."

"May I try?" I asked.

"Certainly."

A lovely senorita was just coming out of her caseta.

"Tell her," I told my friend, "if I were a mule I would pull her carriage from Seville to Cadiz."

My friend transmitted the message and the lady said something in reply.

He returned, "She said it is obvious you do not know the part of the mule a woman sees from a carriage."

Although there is flamenco dancing going on all the time during the feria, the serious dancing starts around two in the morning, when heads are light with wine and hearts are burning from paella.

Senor Koidl, the Austrian manager of the Hotel Alfonso XIII told me, "The Spaniards are slow to open the doors to strangers, but once they open them, they close them behind you and they won't let you go."

No truer words were spoken during the entire feria. The doors were opened for me by the Fierros, a very wealthy and influential Madrid family, whose caseta won first prize for beauty. The Fierros hired the best flamenco dancers in Seville for their caseta, and every morning at two they invited their friends to partake of the festivities.

Imagine, if you will, sitting around an open caseta and exchanging olés with Truman Capote, Cecil Beaton, Ava Gardner, Mrs. Peter Lawford, Mrs. William Woodward, and the couturier Castillo. A man is singing about an eagle who follows a pigeon down to earth and is so smitten with her he can't fly any more.

A bevy of flamenco gypsies are banging their feet against the floor, and everyone is hitting his palms together as the dancers are transported into another world.

Pretty soon the guests get up and do the flamenco. The hours pass by like minutes. Before you know it, it's four in the morning and Ava Gardner is dancing with a gypsy man, just like it says in the movies. Your palms are red from clapping, and you forget about the paella, and the fact that prices have been doubled for the feria, and your wife's luggage has made you one hundred dollars overweight, and her mother is coming over in August.

You're gone, man, gone. But they won't let you go.

The doors are shut. At five your olés are weaker, your carambas stronger. At six your host assures you the fun is just starting. At seven he says the next hour will be the best. At eight he assures you you haven't really seen flamenco, and about nine in the morning, you suddenly find yourself alone in the caseta with the cleaning woman who is sweeping the floor with a castanet.

And that's how it is in Seville during the feria, and if you don't believe me, just ask Ava Gardner who is the American cathedral of us all.

Old Soldiers Never Die

OLD soldiers never die—they just write their memoirs. Ever since the end of World War II, Allied generals and admirals have been writing the story of the war as they saw it. Most of the books seem to indicate that if the author had not been weighted down with political decisions and had been left to fight the war as he saw it, hostilities would have ceased long before 1945. The latest to indicate that he wasn't happy with the way the war was fought was Field Marshal Montgomery, who claims to have differed with General Eisenhower (and even criticized him) in regard to the European campaign.

For thirteen years now publishers have urged me to write my memoirs of World War II. I've been reluctant to do it because there are still many friends who would be hurt at what I have to say. But I've been assured that these memoirs belong to history, and I've been given a large advance on the condition I would make it controversial.

For the first time in any publication, I tell my story of World War II. All rights are reserved and no portion of this story may be reprinted without written permission from General De Gaulle.

In 1942 I received a letter from President Franklin Roosevelt asking me to join the armed services, as the war was going badly and he needed my help. He told me to contact the local draft board, which would make all the necessary arrangements. He felt it would be better for me to deal with the local officials rather than come directly to Washington, where I would only stir up inter-service rivalries over my services.

At the time, I saw a movie called *To the Shores of Tripoli*, and it was obvious the United States Marines needed me.

I was sworn in with the rank of private, but after several months, despite opposition from the Annapolis clique in Marine Corps Headquarters, Washington, I was promoted to private first class, over the heads of many older privates.

President Roosevelt and Winston Churchill had decided the marines would serve in the Pacific theater of operations, and I was put under the joint command of Admiral Nimitz and General MacArthur. In sizing up the situation in the Pacific, I realized that morale was low and I would have to start rebuilding from the bottom.

My strategy at the time was to attack the soft underbelly of Los Angeles and then make a frontal attack on San Francisco. But both Nimitz and MacArthur were for carrying the war to the Japanese *in* the Pacific. I protested to President Roosevelt, through my first sergeant, that this was exactly what the Japanese expected us to do. But General Marshall and Admiral King had President Roosevelt's ear, and he rejected my plan outright. Marshall and King, it turned out, were furious because the President had gone over their heads in inviting me to join the armed services.

I was assigned to Hawaii, which seemed a good place to set up command headquarters. I could keep tabs on the fleet and also supervise island invasions from there. I also started wearing a grass skirt, and every time I appeared in it Division morale went soaring.

Just as I was getting organized, Nimitz and MacArthur decided to send me to Kwajalein Atoll for the invasion. Once again I protested to President Roosevelt. But he had made certain commitments to Churchill and Stalin, and he had to stand by them. The agreement was that if Roosevelt and Churchill would agree to a second front, Stalin would agree to let me attack Kwajalein.

Once again I was sacrificed on the altar of political expediency.

At the last minute, though, it was decided I should attack Eniwetok Atoll instead of Kwajalein. MacArthur was a great and good man, and is now one of my greatest friends, but we were poles apart when it came to the conduct of the war.

My military doctrine was to keep the enemy unbalanced by not knowing where I was. In that way he'd have to commit his reserves, at which time I could send in our Air Force. MacArthur and Nimitz wanted everyone to be fighting all the time. This tragic misunderstanding among the three of us made for indecision and useless expenditure of manpower.

In retrospect, it is obvious that had I been able to attack the soft underbelly of Los Angeles and make my assault on San Francisco (which I was not permitted to do until 1945, when most of the islands were secured), the war in the Pacific would have ended in 1944.

The politicians and the Army and Navy prevented me

from achieving my original goals, and had I known what was going to take place after my entry into the war, I would never have replied to President Roosevelt's original letter.

The Officers' Memoirs Club

ON A RECENT trip to London I was invited to the Officers' Memoirs Club by my good friend, Brigadier Kilt Kooster. The Officers' Memoirs Club, or the OMC as it is known to people in the military trade, is one of the most exclusive clubs in London. It is restricted to retired senior officers who have published at least one book about their war experiences.

When I arrived I found the dining room very crowded, and I was asked to sit down at a table with several friends of Brigadier Kooster.

He introduced me to General Heathwhistle, author of *Thanks for the Memoirs;* Admiral Jaygee, author of *Loose Lips Sank All My Ships;* Colonel Bitters, *How the Germans Could Have Won the War;* Captain Stark Bellows, *The Americans Were Our Enemies;* and Commodore Able Baker-Charley, *Churchill Wouldn't Listen to Me.*

"What news, Kilt Kooster?" General Heathwhistle said.

"Not much. The *Sunday Express* wants to serialize my Italian campaign and the *Reader's Digest* wants me to do a piece on how I found God in Yugoslavia."

"Good show," said Admiral Jaygee. "I think I may have a Book Society Choice with my latest, *The Navy in the Desert.*

"Oh," said Kilt Kooster, "was the Navy in the desert?"

"Not really, but my publishers thought it was a good title. The book is actually about submarines."

Commodore Able Baker-Charley said, "Did you hear old Mintonmouth sold his memoirs to J. Arthur Rank for a packet?"

General Heathwhistle roared, "Good officer, Mintonmouth. I served with him at Brentano's last year. Couldn't say much for his jacket, but the reviews weren't bad. Great man for detail, Mintonmouth. Matter of fact, the book bored me stiff."

Colonel Bitters huffed, "Everybody is writing memoirs these days. My agent says the market's flooded, absolutely flooded. Damn German generals are writing now, and everyone seems to want to read their stories instead of ours."

"Exactly," said Kilt Kooster. "My agent says the same thing. The only place he's been able to sell my last book is Germany. Seems the Germans are fed up with reading books by their generals, and want to read books by us."

"By jove," said Commodore Able Baker-Charley, "why didn't my agent think of that. Naturally Germany is our market. I think I'll switch to MCA."

While we were talking, a very sad-looking man walked by the table. His trembling hand was holding a slip of paper. No one at our table looked up until the man was out of earshot.

"Hailsummer's gotten another rejection slip," Kilt Kooster said.

"It must be his fifteenth."

"Someone should have a talk with him," Colonel Bitters said.

"I've tried," said Admiral Jaygee, "but he won't listen.

He insists on writing that the Americans helped win the war."

"He also says Eisenhower was a good general," Captain Stark Bellows said.

"And worst of all," said Admiral Jaygee, "he attacks Rommel."

"No wonder he can't sell his book," Kilt Kooster added.

"The man," said General Heathwhistle, "shows absolutely no respect for the enemy."

"It's a shame," said Captain Stark Bellows. "Hailsummer's not a bad writer, but he just doesn't know what the public wants."

"Perhaps if we found him a ghost writer. Someone who would really pour it on the Americans."

"What about Monty?"

"Monty's off for Russia," said General Heathwhistle, "to see Khrushchev."

Kilt Kooster said, "I say. Now there's an idea for a book. Why didn't I think of that?"

How To Be a Musical Snob

ONCE MORE WITH FEELING, the successful Broadway play, has been made into a film in Paris, with Yul Brynner playing the leading role of a musical conductor. The author of the play and the screenplay is Harry Kurnitz, an amateur musician who occasionally tips thousands of francs to fiddle with the violinists at the Monseigneur cabaret.

Mr. Kurnitz has studied musical conductors all his life

and told me, "Conducting is the only profession this side of the Iron Curtain where a man can achieve absolute power over his fellow men. Every conductor has a dictator complex, and every dictator probably has a conductor's complex. If only Khrushchev, Tito, Franco, Nasser, and Trujillo had been given symphony orchestras to conduct, what a lot of woe the world might have been saved."

"Isn't it possible for a man to be a good conductor and not be a dictator?"

"No. Musicians like friendly conductors. The only trouble is they won't play for them."

Mr. Kurnitz said that in the last ten years classical music was getting to be an important part of social standing. Even people who don't listen to classical music like to talk about it. He is working on an aid book for such people, so they can keep on top of the table conversation.

"What marks a person more than anything is the composers he discusses. The best ones of course are either the very old or the very new. The man who brings up Vivaldi, instead of Beethoven, is the man to watch."

"You mean if you want to be in the upper crust you must not discuss Beethoven?"

"You can discuss Beethoven quartets, but not the symphonies."

"What about Bach?"

"You can bring up Bach only to work the conversation around to Buxtehude, who was Bach's forerunner."

"How would you do it?" I asked Mr. Kurnitz.

"You might say 'I have nothing against Bach personally, but give me a Buxtehude mass any time.' "

Mr. Kurnitz said that Brahms was definitely non-U (unfashionable) except for the Brahms Clarinet Quintet which, he said, "every jazz clarinetist is knocking his brains out to play these days."

Unfinished works are always fashionable. One man Mr. Kurnitz knows became famous overnight when he wrote a letter to his home-town newspaper complaining that the Board of Directors of the Opera were in a rut because they never put on any new productions. He said he had been trying for a year to get them to produce Franz Schubert's unfinished opera, *Two Friends From Salamanca*, but to no avail. He announced he was forming a musical society known as The Friends of the Two Friends of Salamanca.

He is now considered the foremost expert on opera in his community and has a solid place in the town's musical society.

Musical tastes change, and if one wants to be in instead of out he has to keep up with them. Mr. Kurnitz said, "For years Bartók was fashionable mainly because his music was never played. Then all of a sudden he became the rage—and now musical buffs consider him old hat. Fortunately he died before it happened and never knew the disgrace."

As far as singers go, one must be very careful in discussing them or one might give himself away. "When talking about Maria Callas and Renata Tebaldi you have to be very careful. In order to be considered an expert you can discuss Miss Callas' singing, but *never* her off-stage antics. On the other hand, you can discuss Miss Tebaldi's off-stage antics, but never her singing."

Mr. Kurnitz added, "All music festivals are non-U except Spoleto, Italy, where you have to be a mountain goat to get there."

"What about music from movies?"

"Movie music is so non-U it is almost U."

The yardstick in music for the person starting out to be a connoisseur, Mr. Kurnitz said, is whether something is successful or not. "Success," he told us, "means acceptance; acceptance means the public likes it. If the public likes it it isn't worth talking about. Van Cliburn is a perfect example of this. Before Van Cliburn went to Russia no one heard of him. You could drop his name at a dinner party and everyone sat up and took notice. Now if you mention Van Cliburn's name you're asked to leave the table."

One more word of advice Mr. Kurnitz added, "It's much more fashionable to hate a piece of music than to like it—unless everyone else hates it. But in most cases, when discussing music you have to play it by ear."

The Latest Thing in Abstract Art

THE ultimate in abstract art has been reached. This sounds like a pretty wild statement, and it probably isn't true—but who will remember I said it a year from now? A young sculptor by the name of Jean Tinguely has invented a machine, or several machines, to make abstract paintings. For a dollar, which is what he expects to charge, you can paint your own abstract, as good as anything on the market today, and no one will be able to criticize it.

Mr. Tinguely, who was born in Basel thirty-four years ago, is the inventor of immaterialization, "the hanging from the ceiling of electrical motors which actuate objects and sculpture at very high speeds so that they become immaterialized," and the discoverer of meta-mechanism, which "enables the functional use of hazard."

The importance of meta-mechanism is the secret behind the Do-It-Yourself abstract paintings. Mr. Tinguely believes everyone is an artist at heart, and his machines will be able to help everyone create a work of art.

I found Mr. Tinguely through the aid of Alexander Watt, an art critic who is interested in what Mr. Tinguely is trying to do. Mr. Tinguely lives in a lean-to shack among other lean-to shacks hidden behind Rue Vaugirard—a sculptor colony founded by Brancusi. A public housing project will soon destroy the colorful area.

On the walls of Mr. Tinguely's lean-to were many electric mobiles and on the floor and tables were the meta-matic machines, wired together, all painted black, and each with a long wire arm at the end of which was a clamp where different colored pencils or oil pens could be inserted. Next to the arm was a paper holder. A small electric motor was attached to the body of the machine.

After the person inserts the color he wants, he turns on the current, and the arm starts moving crazily across the paper.

By changing the speeds of the machine and the colors of the crayons, the painting is created in an average time of ten minutes.

Mr. Tinguely insists that his machine share the credit with the person who uses it, and instead of a signature each painting is stamped Painting Executed in Collaboration with Meta-matic Machine No. . . ."

"This," explained Mr. Tinguely, "is an anti-machine ma-

chine, because it does not do the same thing twice. It is also an anti-abstract machine, because it proves anyone can make an abstract painting, even a machine.

"Everyone has an artistic sense, but many people don't have courage to express themselves. My machines will revolutionize the entire art world."

Mr. Tinguely's machines are all different shapes and forms. Some are only capable of working in India ink, others in charcoal, and still others in crayon. A person with fifteen dollars and a couple of hours to spare could make enough abstracts to hold an exhibition.

Mr. Watt showed me an abstract painting he had done on Machine No. 6, which he called an "Early Watt," since it had been done on the previous day.

I made several within the hour while I was interviewing Mr. Tinguely. Mr. Watt, the art critic was very much impressed with the paintings I did on Meta-matic Machine No. 9 and felt my pictures showed warmth, color, and style. I was so happy I almost cut off my left ear.

Speaking of machines, a friend of mine has finally discovered how to beat the billing systems. Many companies throughout the world are now billing their customers on perforated business machine cards untouched by human hands.

My friend found himself being billed for a national magazine he had tried to cancel, but to no avail. Every month he received the same bill on a card, and every month he returned the card with a letter insisting he no longer wanted the magazine, finally becoming pretty nasty about it.

You can't hurt the feelings of a machine, and again he received the same perforated bill. But this time our friend kept his temper. Instead of writing another letter he took a pair of scissors and cut an extra perforation in the card and then sent it back. He hasn't received a magazine or heard from the company since.

A Quiz Program in Russia

THE Union of Soviet Socialist Republics now has about 1,500,000 television sets in operation. So it won't be long before they have quiz programs (the ultimate in TV entertainment).

Here is what a Russian TV quiz program might be like.

The master of ceremonies, Serge Uzbeks, comes out and while an assistant director holds up a large white card for the studio audience, "APPLAUD OR ELSE," he takes a bow and says, "Good evening, comrades. Welcome to 'I Have No Secrets,' the revolutionary new quiz game brought to you by the friendly collective farmers of Kazakhstan, Kirghizia, Uzbekistan, Turkmenia, and Tajikistan. Who is our first contestant, Pavlov?"

"It's Comrade Vashia Bashkiria."

"Comrade Bashkiria, what do you do for a living?"

"I'm a shock worker in a shock absorber factory."

"All right. Comrade Bashkiria, here is your first question. It has to do with Russian cities. The following cities were named after a famous Russian patriot. Give us his first and last name. Here are the cities: Stalingrad, Stalinabad, Stalinogrod, Stalino, and Stalinsk."

"I think it's Josef Stalin."

"I'm sorry, Comrade Bashkiria, the answer is wrong. The cities were named after our great leader, V. I. Lenin."

Two MVD men lead Bashkiria off the stage as the studio audience boos and hisses.

"Who is our next contestant, Pavlov?"

"Comrade Maria Arkhangelskaya."

"What do you do for a living, Comrade Arkhangelskaya?"

"I am Commissar of the Regional Committee for Socialist Productivity of Stall Feeding of Cattle."

(Applause from the audience.)

"All right, comrade, here is your question, in three parts: In 1492 a certain person sailed from a port to prove that the world was round. Instead he discovered America. What was his name, what port did he sail from, and what kind of ship did he sail in?"

"His name was Polino Zvereva, he sailed from Murmansk, and he used an icebreaker."

"That's correct. You have just won the dream of every Russian woman, a brand new six-gear wheat harvester."

(Applause from the audience.)

The tractor is driven on stage and Comrade Arkhangelskaya screams with delight.

"Would you like to continue or stop at the harvester?"

"I would like to continue."

"All right, comrade, here is your next question: Who is the commissar of the Bykova Kitchen Garden Brigade?"

"It is Yevdokia Skorobogatova."

"I'm sorry. Skorobogatova was commissar last week. But it was discovered she was a bourgeois capitalist reactionary imperialist warmonger, and the correct answer is Klavdia Kashkina."

The two MVD men come on stage and drag Maria off.

"What about my harvester?" she screams.

"You won't need it where you're going."

(Assistant director holds up card, "LAUGH OR ELSE.")

Off-stage the sounds of shots are heard.

The M.C. smiles. "Well, you can't win them all." Then, "Pavlov we have time for one more contestant."

"Comrade Ivan Ivanov."

"What is your profession, comrade?"

"I am a member of the Secret Police."

The M. C. goes white.

Then he says, "Comrade Ivanov, you have just won the Dniepropetrovsk Iron and Steel Works."

"You haven't asked me a question."

"I know you know the answer, so why should I ask?"

"Ask the question."

"It would only be a formality, Comrade Ivanov. Why should I use up your time?"

"ASK THE QUESTION!"

"Pppp lll eee ase tttell us who the the the cccity of Lennnn iinnnggg rrad was nnammed after?"

"Josef Stalin."

"That's correct," the M.C. shouts.

"I thought so," the secret policeman says. He takes out a revolver. "Stalin was an enemy of the people." He fires six bullets into the M.C. As the M.C. slumps to the floor, the audience applauds.

An announcer comes on and says, "That's all for this

week, comrades. Tune in next week to 'I Have No Secrets,' same time, same station, different master of ceremonies."

Paris Is Going To Be Destroyed

PARIS is going to be destroyed in a new monster movie now in preparation. The picture will be made by the King Brothers, Maury, Frank, and Hyman, who told me they make inexpensive movies look like expensive ones. I had breakfast with Maury and Frank at the Hotel George V (Hyman was home working on the monsters), and the brothers said their latest endeavor could be compared in scope, but not necessarily in subject matter, with *The Ten Commandments*.

"The picture is called *Gorgo*," said Maury, "which is also the name of our monsters."

"It's not one monster," Frank interrupted. "It's two monsters. A baby monster and a mama monster."

"But," said Frank, "they're not monsters as we think of monsters. I mean, they're not mean monsters. They destroy Paris but they don't mean to do it."

"I think, we better start at the beginning," I said.

"Well," said Maury, "we open up in the Pacific with these two fishermen, Joe and Sam, who have been thrown off course by an earthquake."

"It isn't the earthquake which throws them off course," Frank said. "It's the tidal wave that comes after the earthquake."

"That's right," Maury agreed. "Now, while they're fish-ing, suddenly out of the ocean comes a baby monster seventy-five feet high."

"One hundred feet high," Frank corrected.

"Yeh, one hundred feet high. It looks like a giant lizard. But it's not a mean-looking lizard. It's a friendly-looking lizard."

"The eyes are very sad," Frank said. "You immediately have sympathy for it."

"Well," continued Maury, "one of the fishermen, Joe, is always looking for a fast buck and he says they should take the monster back to Paris and show it at the circus."

"Why Paris?"

"Well, that's where we want to make the picture," Maury said.

"That's where Maury wants to make the picture," Frank said, "I'd rather make it in Australia, where we can get a better deal.

"Yeh," Maury said, "but there are no monuments in Australia, and besides, who cares if a monster destroys Australia? It's the fact that the monster is going to destroy Paris that's important."

"I still say," said Frank, "it's too expensive to make in France."

"Gentlemen, please," I begged, "the story."

"Well, the good fisherman Sam wants to throw the monster back into the water, but his partner prevails and they bring it to Paris, where it's a big hit. But what they don't know is that this monster is a baby monster and has a mother."

"That makes it a sympathetic monster as far as I'm concerned," I said.

"The mama monster starts looking for the baby monster."

"How can she find him?" I asked.

"Well, the monsters have to live in water and the circus people bathe the baby monster in the Seine. The mama monster can smell her baby, and she swims up the Seine from Le Havre when she gets the scent. It's a very foggy night, so no one sees her. She's two hundred feet long."

"Two hundred and fifty feet," Frank said.

"She doesn't want to destroy Paris," Maury explains. "She's just looking for her baby. Everyone is rooting for her."

"But in trying to find her baby," Frank said, "she wrecks the Eiffel Tower, the Arc de Triomphe, the Louvre, the Opéra, the Grand Palais, and two bridges on the Seine."

"We also might have her wreck Fouquet's café," Maury said, "because they charge too much."

"Now for the finish. The monster is descending on Notre Dame and just as she is about to destroy it she finds her baby."

"Then Notre Dame isn't destroyed?"

"It's like a miracle," Frank said.

"And then," said Maury, "the baby monster and the mama monster go back into the Seine and swim out to sea."

"You see," said Frank, "most monsters are killed at the end of the picture. But this is going to be different. Our star is the monster. She didn't want to destroy Paris."

"We're going to destroy Paris like it's never been destroyed before," Maury said. "Frank's dying to, because of the prices. But Paris has something. Tokyo's already been destroyed; so has Berlin. And King Kong wrecked New York. Paris is one of the few places left that hasn't been wrecked."

"You didn't tell him about the voice of morality in the picture." Frank said.

"That's right. We got this young kid. He's the salt of the earth. His father's been killed by the monster but he holds no grudges. He says if you leave monsters alone, they'll leave you alone. That's the message of the picture."

"I still think," Frank said, "we should make it in Australia."

I was on Frank's side, but I didn't have the nerve to interfere.

Life Presents a Dismal Picture

I WAS invited up to Oxford to take part in a debate sponsored by the Oxford Union, the most famous debating society in the world. The subject was "This House Proposes That Life Presents a Dismal Picture." They really wanted Charles Van Doren to speak for the motion, but when he wasn't available they tried to get the president of the American cranberry industry. Finally they asked me if I would take on the pro side of the debate, on the theory I could present as dismal a picture as any American in these parts.

It was a very flattering invitation and one I didn't hesitate to accept. For one thing the Oxford Union Society, founded in 1823, is a training ground for future British politicians. Youths who have spoken there have gone on to be Prime

Ministers of the country as well as members of Parliament. Scouts from the Conservative, Labour, and Liberal parties are on hand at every debate, hoping to find another Gladstone, Hilaire Belloc, or Harold Macmillan.

Perhaps, I thought, somebody from the Conservative party will spot me and ask me to run against Bessie Braddock in Liverpool. If Pete Dawkins could win his blue as a rugby player at Oxford, it wouldn't be too farfetched for me to become the next Prime Minister of England.

Besides that, I reasoned, it was the obligation of every adult to help young people and bring to them words of comfort, encouragement, and hope. Students are confused and seeking wisdom from those of us who have been subjected to the blows of the cruel world.

Therefore, with a light heart, I jotted a few thoughts down on some cards, bought a round-trip ticket from Paddington Station to Oxford, and went forth to address these young, fresh minds, who I was sure were waiting to hear every pearl I was going to drop.

The Oxford Union is fraught with tradition. The president, Mr. Joseph Trattner, wears white tie and tails, as do the secretary and treasurer. The hall for the debate is a replica of the House of Commons, and the debaters, in tuxedos, sit on benches on each side of the president.

The audience, composed of the cream of Oxford intellectual society, sit on benches downstairs, while females and other guests are seated in the galleries.

The debate got under way at 8:45 P.M. There were two students on my side—Mr. Jack Hazelgrove and Mr. Paul Foot, son of Sir Hugh Foot. Opposing the motion were Brian Walsh, brought in from Cambridge for the evening,

Mr. Ivan Lawrence, a student, and Mr. H. E. Ellis, an editorial director of *Punch*.

The students were to speak first, and each one, bucking for a future Cabinet post, had worked on his speech for months. Every thrust was met with hilarious applause. They had inserted satirical digs at politicians, the clergy, and the Empire. They slashed away at members of Parliament and professors at Oxford. They used Joycean puns, and they did imitations of their leaders. They were playing for keeps, and the laughter was frightening to hear.

By the time the third student speaker was halfway through I started to think of ways of getting out of the hall. I couldn't make a dash for the door because it was blocked. I then thought of getting sick and passing out. The white cards I held in my hands started to turn to pulp.

References were made in Latin which got laughs, philosophers I had never heard of were referred to and broke the place up. The only thing I could think of was a bullfight; the student speakers were the matadors and the guest speakers were the bulls.

All I could hope for was a quick, clean death.

What made it worse was that each speaker, in turn, assured the audience he was only warming up the audience for the guest speakers. Ellis looked a little pale too, and I tried to pass a note to him suggesting we escape together out the window. But the president caught the note and tore it up.

Finally they called on me. I staggered to the speaker's box and in a faint voice grabbed the water and asked, "Is this safe to drink?" They laughed. Little did they know I was on the verge of fainting.

The rest of the speech remains a blur. Does the bull know what the crowd shouts from the stands?

Somehow the evening ended, and the final vote was taken. The students voted 232 to 221 against us. Life to them was not a dismal picture. It was a blow to me that I doubt I'll ever recover from. By losing the debate I loused up my chances of ever becoming Prime Minister of England.

Person to Person

WHEN Dr. Frank Stanton, the president of the Columbia Broadcasting System, came out for honesty on television, one of the first programs he said had to be cleaned up was *Person to Person*. It seems that *Person to Person*, a program that interviews people in their homes, was rehearsed, and it was revealed that the people were talked to in advance of the show. This, said Dr. Stanton, was fooling the public, who were under the impression that Ed Murrow, the interviewer, just walked into somebody's living room with a television camera over his shoulder and started talking to his guests right away.

Well, I'm happy to report that *Person to Person* is now clean as a hound's tooth, and there is no more of this undercover stuff in the kitchen before the show goes on the air. At the end of each program a voice announces, "The production of *Person to Person* has involved advance planning with the guest as to what to show and what to discuss."

I know all this because I did *Person to Person* in our home one Saturday. It was taped for showing in the United States later. But what Dr. Stanton doesn't know is that while his crew did the show on the up and up, attempts were made before that Saturday to "fix" the program. The fact the attempt failed was only due to the reluctance of certain members of the household to become part of it.

What happens when you are scheduled to appear on *Person to Person* is that first you are visited by the director, writer, and producer of the show. The director studies the house from the best camera angles, the writer interviews you so he can give Mr. Charles Collingwood, who took Mr. Murrow's place as M. C., leading questions to ask the family. The producer is there to assure you that if anything is broken *Person to Person* will pay for the damage.

During the conference it was decided we'd open up with the children eating dinner. Mr. Collingwood would interview the children about food, and then we would show him the apartment. It seemed simple, honest, and forthright, and a program that the broadcasting industry could be proud of.

But as soon as the director, writer, and producer left, I said to my wife, "We'll serve the children a cheese soufflé, filet mignon, French fried potatoes, and crêpes suzette."

"But," she protested, "the children don't eat that for dinner."

"I'm not going to have people all over America think we starve our children," I said.

Then we called in our six-year-old son, our five-year-old daughter, and our three-year-old daughter.

I said, "Children, a nice man is going to come to the house and make television pictures on Saturday morning, and he's going to speak to all of you."

They nodded.

"Now he's going to ask you what you like to eat, and do you know what you're going to tell him?"

My son said, "Peanut butter and pickles."

My five-year-old daughter said, "Mashed potatoes and chewing gum."

And my three-year-old said, "I'm not hungry, I don't want to eat anything."

"Hah," my wife said.

"That's very nice," I said patiently. "But when the nice man asks you what you like to eat you must say 'cheese soufflé.' "

My son said, "What's a cheese soufflé?"

"It's a cake," I said, "only softer."

"I don't want a soufflé!" my five-year-old shouted.

The three-year-old screamed, "I don't want a soufflé! I don't want a soufflé! I want a rabbit, a dog, and a doll house!"

"I think you'd better try something else," my wife suggested.

"Shut up," I said to all of them, losing my temper. "You'll love it when you taste it. Now the nice man is going to ask you other questions, too. He's going to ask you what you like best about school. What will you reply?"

"A cheese soufflé," my son said immediately.

"No," I said, "You like speaking French. That's what you like about school."

"That's silly," my five-year-old said. "I don't want to be on television. I want to be in the cinema."

"I don't want to be on television," the three-year-old shouted, getting red in the face. "I don't want to be on television. I want to be a witch."

The conference was called to a halt, and I decided to proceed without further discussion.

Saturday came. Millions of cables, machines, cameras, and technicians filled the house, and at two thirty in the afternoon we were ready to shoot the "dinner scene." The children hadn't been fed since eight o'clock in the morning, on my orders, and as I guessed, they dived into the cheese soufflé and lapped it up as if it was whipped cream.

The cameras were rolling, and Mr. Collingwood said to my son, "What are you eating, Joel?"

Joel looked up and said, "Roast beef."

It's kids like this, Dr. Stanton, that are going to save television.

The Backfield in Motion

THE Windmill Theatre (We Never Closed), located in the heart of London, has the distinction of presenting seminude musical revues for twenty-seven years without interruption. It is not a burlesque house—it does not feature strip-teasers—and except for the fact that the girls go through their numbers with very little on, there is nothing offensive about the show.

Because of this, and the fact that it was the only theater to stay open during the dark days of the Blitz, the Windmill has a warm place in the hearts of many Britishers.

The clientele is composed of men, the majority middle-aged and older, with just a sprinkling of soldiers and sailors here and there. What most people are unaware of is that there is a sport involved in attending a Windmill show and one that requires great skill and courage—qualities the British are not lacking. There is a saying that "The battle of the Suez Canal was won on the playing fields of the Windmill Theatre."

In order to find out more about the sport I went to the Windmill with a Mr. James Hanson, foxhunter, yachtsman, horse-racing enthusiast, and an inveterate theatergoer. Mr. Hanson said he felt that since World War II, the Americans had ignored the sport of Windmill-going, and he hoped we could revive it.

"Briefly," he explained to me on the way to the theater, "the sport is played as follows: The Windmill Theatre has a continuous show that starts at noon and runs until ten thirty in the evening. There are no reserved seats. The object of the game is for the player who starts in the last row to get to the front row which, as you can guess, is the best place for this type of show. Since everyone in the theater is trying to get a seat in the first row, you can imagine how difficult it is. What makes the sport even more hazardous is that climbing over the seats is strictly forbidden."

It sounded very interesting, and I was anxious to play.

When we arrived at the theater there was a large sign at the cashier's window, which read: "No Artificial Aid to Vision Permitted." This included binoculars and explained why everyone wanted to sit in the first row.

After buying our tickets and presenting them to the doorman we were told to go downstairs to the theater. I was just about to check my coat in the cloakroom when Mr. Hanson stopped me. "There are two schools of thought on checking your coat. One says you can move faster unencumbered, but I'm of the school that believes a coat can come in handy as a weapon to trip up an opponent. Besides, although there is a rule about climbing over a seat, there is nothing in the books about throwing your coat over one. If I were you, I'd hold on to it."

You can't argue with the coach, so I kept my coat. As we entered the theater we found it full, except for the last few rows. On stage, several scantily clad English lasses were complaining in song about a tropical heat wave.

Mr. Hanson took me to the back and told me there was no chance of making a move until the number was over.

"No one leaves," he explained, "while the girls are on the stage. But don't relax; you never know when the curtain is coming down."

Things looked kind of blurred in the last row and I was straining to see what was going on.

Suddenly the curtain went down and Mr. Hanson said, "Now!"

I jumped up and rushed down two more rows and grabbed an aisle seat that had just been vacated by someone who had moved on down.

"Your form is all right," Mr. Hanson said, "but you should have been in the seat faster. You stood up to let somebody out. Don't do that; you can get hurt. Now take out your cigarette lighter."

"What for?"

"Nudes on a London stage must remain stationary unless the lights are dimmed. Watch this."

Sure enough, a nude was dancing around under dark blue lights and the theater was ablaze with light as everyone pretended he was lighting a cigarette.

"The comedian goes on after this number," Hanson said, "and the theater usually empties out pretty fast. With any luck, we'll make four rows."

The number was over and we made a dash for it. One row, two rows, three rows, and we were at the fourth row when someone shoved me aside.

"Use your coat," Hanson cried.

I threw my coat over the man's head, pushed him aside, and made it to the seat. While I held down a seat for Hanson, he retrieved the coat.

"That was a dangerous play," he lectured me. "Never let go of your coat or you may not get it back. We had a close call. If we hadn't made it, we would have had to start all over again. As you can see, someone has grabbed our previous seats."

I was beginning to appreciate the skill required in the game.

As time went on I became more proficient. I learned how to trip an opponent, sit on his hat, and force him through a fire exit.

We only had to sit through three shows before we found ourselves in the first row with nothing but the orchestra pit separating us from the girls on the stage. I was so elated I started to take a bow, but Hanson pushed me down in the seat.

"For heaven's sake," he said, "sit down before someone steals the seat right out from under you."

As the girls started dancing with fans, Hanson took a

stop watch out of his pocket. "We made it in three hours ten minutes twenty-three seconds."

"Why that's shorter than *Ben Hur*," I couldn't help shouting.

Hanson admitted it wasn't bad for a beginner, but he warned me against overconfidence.

"Better men than you thought they had the sport made after one try, and do you know where they are today? Up there," he said, "up there sitting with crutches in the balcony."

Question of the Scoubidou

Now I'll take up the question of the scoubidou. Frankly I've been trying to avoid the subject, hoping it would go away. But at the moment the scoubidou (pronounced skoo-bee-do) in France is bigger than all of us and there isn't a French child in the country who hasn't made, bought, or sold a scoubidou.

The scoubidou has two characteristics which seemed to guarantee its success among French children: it's of no use whatsoever, and nobody knows exactly what the word means. There is also a verb in French now *to scoubidou*, which describes the action of making a scoubidou.

To scoubidou you braid two or four plastic electric wires, usually two to four inches long, and leave a loop on top so it can fit on a key chain or on a schoolbag or on a pin that can be placed on a sweater. The braiding is complicated, requiring dexterity, and speed. The skill needed is complicated by the fact that most of the French children do their scoubidouing in school, during classes, and if caught their scoubidous are confiscated by the teacher.

The contest between teacher and pupil has contributed to the popularity of the scoubidou, and it is estimated by experts that only one out of four scoubidous made in class is confiscated. This has led to scoubidou competitions in classrooms. The student who makes the longest scoubidou during one class period wins.

The scoubidou craze has had an amazing effect on the electrical industry. In the beginning the run on electric wire was too much for many supply stores and almost brought serious electrical wiring to a standstill. Since then the department stores have stocked up on the plastic covering for wire without the metal inside. This was a boon to scoubidouing. It also saved most French families from doing without electricity, as the run on wiring in homes was getting serious.

An interesting thing is that bakeries where candy is sold have suffered in the last three months because all the French children's pocket money has been going for wire and not for bonbons. To stop this loss of business the bakeries now sell candies and electric wires in the same package.

One candy manufacturer tried to sell candy and *ready-made* scoubidous in the same package, but this flopped. Apparently French children have no interest in a scoubidou unless they make it themselves.

We were very fortunate to have an exclusive interview with Monsieur Vincent Sidem, aged twelve, who is considered by his friends to be a maître scoubidouist. M. Sidem, who was wearing four scoubidous on his belt like scalps, has made a commercial success out of the craze. He has an American uncle who recently had a heart attack in Paris. The scoubidou is supposed to have good luck qualities, and while his uncle was recovering, he offered to buy any scoubidous that his nephew could make.

M. Sidem immediately invested money in plastic wire, which he distributed among his friends and made a killing by selling three dozen scoubidous to his uncle within a week.

But M. Sidem said his uncle expects to go back to America in a few days and so he has slowed up production and the ordering of wire, as Paris is virtually flooded with scoubidous, and unless you have an uncle recovering from a heart attack it's very difficult to find customers.

A boy's ability to make a good scoubidou doesn't necessarily raise his standing in the eyes of other boys. "Everyone knows it won't last too long," he said, "and you're still better off if you can play soccer."

He said he foresees in the not too distant future the day when you'll be laughed out of class for making a scoubidou. He blamed Christmas for this.

"Everyone made scoubidous for Christmas presents," he explained, thus flooding the market and speeding up the demise of scoubidouing before its time.

Another factor is that a scoubidou, once made, lasts a lifetime, and since it doesn't wear out, there will be less and less demand for new ones. M. Sidem and his friends can't conceive of the scoubidou surviving the winter. It is being picked up in Belgium and Holland though, and may reach Scandinavia by summertime.

As for a scoubidou becoming a craze in America, no one knows. The French children never did take the hula hoop seriously, and it's quite possible that American children, in retaliation, may ignore the scoubidou.

It's one of those perfect chacun à son goût situations.

7. The Yellow American

Let's See Who Salutes

HAVE you ever wondered what would have happened if the people who are in charge of television today were passing on the draft of the Declaration of Independence?

The scene is Philadelphia at WJULY TV. Several men are sitting around holding copies of the Declaration.

Thomas Jefferson comes in nervously.

"Tommy," says the producer, "it's just great. I would say it was a masterpiece."

"We love it, Tommy boy," the advertising agency man says. "It sings. Lots of drama, and it holds your interest. There are a few things that have to be changed, but otherwise it stays intact."

"What's wrong with it?" Mr. Jefferson asks.

There's a pause. Everyone looks at the man from the network.

"Well, frankly, Tommy, it smacks of being a little anti-British. I mean, we've got quite a few British listeners and something like this might bring in a lot of mail."

"Now don't get sore, Tommy boy," the agency man says. "You're the best declaration of independence writer in the business. That's why we hired you. But our sponsor the Boston Tea Company is interested in selling tea, not independence. Mr. Cornwallis, the sponsor's representative, is here, and I think he has a few thoughts on the matter. Go ahead, Corney. Let's hear what you think."

Mr. Cornwallis stands up. "Mr. Jefferson, all of us in this room want this to be a whale of a document. I think we'll agree on that."

Everyone in the room nods his head.

"At the same time we feel—I think I can speak for everybody—that we don't want to go over the heads of the mass of people who we hope will buy our product. You use words like despotism, annihilation, migration, and tenure. Those are all egghead words and don't mean a damn thing to the public. Now I like your stuff about 'Life, Liberty, and the pursuit of Happiness.' They all tie in great with tea, particularly pursuit of happiness, but it's the feeling of all of us that you're really getting into controversial water when you start attacking the King of Britain."

Mr. Jefferson says, "But every word of it is true. I've got documentary proof."

"Let me take a crack at it, Corney," the agency man says. "Look, Tommy boy, it isn't a question of whether it's true or not. All of us here know what a louse George can be. But I don't think the people want to be reminded of it all the time. They have enough worries. They want escape. This thing has to be upbeat. If you remind people of all those taxes George has laid on us, they're not going to go out and buy tea. They're not going to go out and buy anything."

"Frankly," says the network man, "I have some strong objections on different grounds. I know you didn't mean it this way, but the script strikes me as pretty left-wing. I may have read the last paragraph wrong, but it seems to me that you're calling for the overthrow of the present government by force. The network could never allow anything like that."

SOAP

"I'm sure Tommy didn't mean anything like that," the producer says. "Tommy's just a strong writer. Maybe he got a little carried away with himself. Suppose Tommy took out all references to the British and the King. Suppose we said in a special preamble this Declaration of Independence had nothing to do with persons living or dead, and the whole thing is fictitious. Wouldn't that solve it?"

Mr. Jefferson says, "Gentlemen, I was told to write a Declaration of Independence. I discussed it with many people before I did the actual writing. I've worked hard on this declaration—harder than I've worked on anything in my life. You either take it or leave it as it is."

"We're sorry you feel that way about it, Tommy," the agency man says. "We owe a responsibility to the country, but we owe a bigger responsibility to the sponsor. He's paying for it. We're not in the business of offending people, British people or any other kind of people. The truth is, the British are the biggest tea drinkers of anyone in the colonies. We're not going to antagonize them with a document like this. Isn't that so, Mr. Cornwallis?"

"Check—unless Mr. Jefferson changes it the way we want him to."

Mr. Jefferson grabs the Declaration and says, "Not for all the tea in China," and exits.

The producer shakes his head. "I don't know, fellows. Maybe we've made a mistake. We could at least have run it up a flagpole to see who saluted."

"As far as I'm concerned," Mr. Cornwallis said, "the subject is closed. Let's talk about an hour Western on the French and Indian War."

Helpful Phrases for Western Conferences

One of the problems of a meeting between President De Gaulle and President Eisenhower is the language problem. General De Gaulle speaks a little English and President Eisenhower speaks a little French. But since these talks are so important, the two leaders may have a problem getting through the rugged sessions which lie ahead.

I have been working on an English-French phrase book for just such a meeting, and perhaps it will be helpful to the two principals involved.

First, here are some practical English phrases for General De Gaulle.

AT THE AIRPORT

Good day, my dear President. How are you? (*Bonjour, Monsieur le Président. Comment allez-vous, Monsieur le Président?*)

Have you anything to declare? (*Avez-vous quelque-chose à déclarer?*)

Can I cash travelers' checks at the Quai d'Orsay? (*Peut-on toucher des chèques de voyage au Quai d'Orsay?*)

I have only two nights. Can you recommend a good restaurant? (*Je ne reste que deux jours. Pourriez-vous me recommander un bon restaurant?*)

I hear that Paris is very expensive. (*On me dit que Paris est atrocement cher.*)

Monty says hello. (*Le Maréchal Montgomery m'a chargé

de vous transmettre, Monsieur le Président, l'expression de sa haute considération.)

Where can I buy a fountain pen for my wife? (*Où est la plume de ma femme?*)

AT THE ELYSEE
(*The important talks*)

For General De Gaulle:

How is everything in Little Rock? (*Comment ça marche à Little Rock?* [*au Petit Rocher*])

President Eisenhower:

Comment vont les affaires d'Algérie? (How is everything in Algeria?)

General De Gaulle:

Touché. (*No translation*)

President Eisenhower:

Est-ce que l'année est bonne pour le vin? (How was the wine crop this year?)

General De Gaulle:

It will be a great year. (*C'est une année dont on se souviendra.*)

President Eisenhower:

Encore une chose. (There is one more thing.)

General De Gaulle:

Yes (*Oui.*)

President Eisenhower:

Comment faut-il faire pour traduire Fahrenheit en Centigrade? (How do you translate Fahrenheit into Centigrade?)

General De Gaulle:

I will tell you if you give us the bomb. (*Je vous donnerai la clef si vous nous donnez la bombe.*)

President Eisenhower:

J'ai promis au congrès de ne pas le faire. (I promised Congress I wouldn't.)

General De Gaulle:

Then there is really nothing more to talk about. (*En ce cas nous n'avons plus rien à nous dire.*)

President Eisenhower:

Vous pouvez peut-être m'indiquer l'heure du départ de l'autobus pour Chartres? (Could you tell me when the next bus leaves for Chartres?)

Wake Up, America

(While I was on vacation, I asked Joseph Wallstop, syndicated columnist, political commentator, and authority on world affairs, what was happening in world affairs. His report, which follows, is very pessimistic.)

I HAVE just returned from an extensive visit to Lovlost-by-the-Sea, and I have never been more depressed since World War II ended. In the battle for men's minds we have overlooked one of the key powers in the free world, and, if something isn't done immediately, the Russians will take over and we will find ourselves without a friend in this bastion of liberty and free enterprise.

In order to understand the dire predicament the West faces in Lovlost, I talked to the leading politicians and statesmen in the country, and they all came to the same conclusion. Unless the country received immediate financial aid from the United States it would become a Communist satellite.

Lovlost's troubles started in 1950. Up until then she received $300,000,000,000 a year from the United States under the Marshall Plan. Her industry thrived, there was no unemployment, and her people had one of the highest standards of living in Europe.

Then the blow fell. Lovlost ran out of Communists. While Lovlost had Communists (the 1949 elections showed she had twelve) the United States was willing to underwrite any program Lovlost wanted. All the Lovlost Foreign Minister had to do was to go to Washington and point out that these twelve Communists could take over the country at any moment, and the State Department would give him all the money he could carry back on his ship (a new aircraft carrier which was supposed to go to France, but somehow got lost in transit).

But in the 1950 elections the twelve Communists, who had become rich on Marshall Aid, voted for the Right-wing Conservative Republican Party.

When the returns were in, the State Department was horrified. Lovlost had betrayed the experts who had predicted Lovlost was on the verge of going Red. Congress, which had voted the money, was outraged. The head of the Senate Finance Committee said, "We've been taken for a ride. We gave Lovlost millions of the taxpayer's money because we thought they were threatened by the Communists, and now it turns out they have NO Communists." There was an uproar in the newspapers. It happened at the time of the McCarthy hysteria and the headlines screamed, "MORE REDS IN STATE DEPARTMENT THAN IN LOVLOST—AMERICANS BETRAYED."

Word got back to Lovlost, and it was decided to hold another election. The Prime Minister begged the twelve Communists to vote the Communist ticket, but they refused. "We don't believe in Marxism any more," the former leader of the party said. "Death to Stalin, long live General Motors!"

The Prime Minister asked Russia to lend some Communists, but Russia said as long as they accepted American aid it was impossible to lend any Communists to Lovlost.

The elections were held and, once again, not a single Communist vote was cast. America immediately cut off her aid in disgust. Since then, without dollars, the country has been going to pot. Factories have closed, homes have been foreclosed, and the Lovlost Lickel is now pegged at eighty-nine hundred to the dollar. The country is ripe for a Russian take-over.

This shocking condition caused by idiotic statesmanship, accented by negligence and stupidity, crawling with omission and frustration, is typical of what has been going on in Washington for the last one hundred eighty-three years.

The alarm flags are up. Lovlost has brought Americans closer to the brink than they have ever been before. There is nothing but complacency on Capitol Hill, and I, for one, predict that unless people wake up to the plain, brutal facts, this reckless policy we have been following will only mean one thing: "Lovlost will be lost."

When I spoke to the Foreign Minister he pleaded with me, "Send us some Communists. We'll even take fellow travelers. We'll even take Paul Robeson. Just anybody who will help us get American aid."

The question every American must answer as he reads

this column is, "Are we willing to lose Lovlost over a few lousy Communists whom we can easily spare, or are we going to close our eyes to the irrevocable truth and say, as we have been saying for the last nine years, 'To hell with Lovlost'?"

The Yellow American

It's pretty hard for a foreigner to keep neutral in the French crisis. It can also be very dangerous. I discovered this last week when I hailed a taxicab at the Place de la Concorde for a trip home. The driver, a very large man who took up most of the front seat, started the conversation as soon as I got in.

"What is the latest news?" he wanted to know.

Thinking I was in the government camp I said, "It looks like De Gaulle is going to have his way."

"Hah," he said, turning to me as he continued driving. "De Gaulle is finished. Monsieur, I was a Gaullist, but I am finished with him. He betrayed the people of Algiers. Everyone in France is against him. He is a——" and then he used a five-letter French word.

"Exactly my feelings," I said hurriedly, hoping he would turn his eyes to the front.

He did for a moment, and I relaxed.

"He should have never let Pinay quit," the driver said.

"Pinay was good for the country," I agreed.

He turned around again. "The new government should be Bidault, General Massu, Marshal Juin, and Pinay."

"A marvelous government," I squeaked, not trying to look ahead.

He looked forward again, but only while we stopped at a red light.

Then he said, "The whole mess was caused by the Americans." He looked hard at me, and we missed a bus by several inches. "If the Americans hadn't stopped us at Suez, Tunisia and Morocco would be French."

"I was saying the same thing to my wife this morning," I said, trying not to notice a heavy truck that was bearing down on us.

The driver swerved just in time.

I picked myself off the floor, breathing hard.

The taxicab driver was working himself up into a rage and he seemed to be trying to pull his steering wheel off the shaft.

As he screeched around a corner he looked around again and said threateningly, "Are you American or English?"

Without hesitation I said, "I'm English."

"They're even worse!" he shouted.

"I'm not really English," I cried. "I'm Australian."

He didn't seem to hear me. "The English are plotting against us with the Germans. They don't want to be part of Europe. Who needs them?"

"I think you're going to hit a monument," I blubbered.

He glanced forward, but only for a second. Then he turned to me and said, "What do the Australians think of this mess?"

"We're all very upset at the moment."

"You should be," he said. "The Americans and the British don't understand our problems. They're against us because of the oil in the Sahara. They know they won't be able to sell their oil once we get ours out of the ground."

"French oil is the crux of the whole matter," I agreed hysterically. "The Americans don't want *you* to have any oil. It's obvious to everybody."

He grunted and then started swearing again. "But don't worry. "We'll take care of all of them."

"Isn't that a metro station you're aiming at?" I asked in what I hoped was a casual way.

He almost drove down the steps.

When he righted the taxi, he said, "Have you talked to any other Frenchmen?"

"Yes."

"Do they say the same thing?"

"Without exception," I said. "They all agree with you."

We finally arrived at my house, and I paid the man, tipping him heavily. He said as he took the money, "I don't like most foreigners, monsieur, but you are different. At least you speak your mind."

The Beep Generation

THE best thing about satellites and rockets is that they can talk, and anyone who knows how to tune in can find out exactly what's going on in their heads. Up until the launching of Pioneer, it was much more convenient for everyone to speak German. But Pioneer, from all reports, was the first one to speak good English.

How do I know this? In reading reports of the launching I saw where one of the scientists was quoted as saying to the Pioneer as it took off, "Go, man, go."

From this, I guessed Pioneer not only spoke English, but was a real hep ball of fire.

My suspicions were verified when I tuned in on the Pioneer wave-length by accident. I was really looking for the Armed Forces Network. Pioneer was talking with Vanguard I, Explorer I, Explorer IV, and Sputnik III.

This is what I heard:

Pioneer: Out of my way, man. I have to go, go, go.

Vanguard I (*faintly*): Where are you going?

Pioneer: Out of this world. I'm doing the moonsville bit. I'm going so far out they'll never find me. I'm the cat that's going to jump over the moon.

Sputnik III: What kind of tail are you spinning?

Pioneer: No tail, man, I'm real gone. Come fly with me, Wheeeee.

Explorer I (*ever so faintly*): You're real high. How did you get so high?

Pioneer: It depends on what you smoke, man. Don't forget I just got off the pad. Go, gogogo. Crazy.

Vanguard I: He's writing his own orbituary.

Explorer IV: I don't know what these young missiles are coming to.

Pioneer: I'm a gasser. Rocket rocket rocket around the clocket.

Vanguard I: I think he's on pot.

Explorer I: They may have put something in his countdown.

Sputnik III: It smells more like vodka to me.

Pioneer: I'm dizzy but not stupid. I love beep but can't stand bop. I gotta go, go, go.

Explorer I: I've been up here a long time, son. And if you keep behaving like that you're going to burn yourself out.

Vanguard I: Just calm yourself and go around quietly the way we're doing.

Pioneer: Hi diddle diddle the cat and the fiddle, the clyde jumped over the moon, the little dog laughed to see such fun, but this is the first time anyone's seen it on television. Would any of you like to buy a commercial?

Explorer IV: Please try to remain cool.

Pioneer: Cool, man. I can't remain cool when I'm going seventy-five hundred miles an hour. I'm the first spitball to the moon.

Explorer I: You look very pale.

Pioneer: I need a booster. Give me a fix, man. Just one little old booster. Please, Please.

Apparently the scientists heard him, because after a few seconds I heard Pioneer say, Whew, I thought I was a goner there for a moment.

Sputnik III: What's a fix?

Pioneer: It's what keeps you out of this world. It makes you go through the roof.

Vanguard I: He'll never go to the moon in the condition he's in.

Explorer IV: Why doesn't he leave well enough alone?

Sputnik III: He needs somebody to love, like a dog.

Pioneer: You're all a bunch of squares. You're not with

it. If you want to be happy you have to radiate. You're all earthbound.

Explorer I: At least we know our orbit and stay in it and don't bother anybody.

Vanguard I: These advanced launching methods are too much for me.

Pioneer: Do you know what I'm going to have for lunch? Green cheese! Yum, yum. One more fix and then I'm off.

Explorer IV: All right already. On your way.

Pioneer: Get on your mark, get set—go, go, go, go, go.

Explorer I: He's gone. Good riddance. If he were mine I'd give him a good padding.

Explorer IV: I can't stand this beep generation.

Vanguard I: They've lost all their sense of values.

Suddenly I heard a crash on the radio.

Explorer I: I told him not to drive so fast.

Confessions of a Russian Agitator

ONE of Russia's chief agitators, Alexandrov Kendrikovitch, has just defected from the U.S.S.R., and for the first time I was able to get a clear picture of what has been going on behind the scenes of Agitprop, the latest in a series of top secret Soviet government espionage agencies.

Alexandrov (that's not his real name of course) told me that ever since the cultural exchanges were set up between the U.S.A. and the U.S.S.R., and the series of visits between high officials of both countries occurred, Agitprop has become a very important organization. His career as a professional agitator was assured until a fatal mistake last week in Scotland. Because of this Alexandrov had to defect. But I'm getting ahead of the story.

"It was a good job," Alexandrov told me sadly, "and I made a living. But as East-West relations thawed, the work got harder, and more demands were made on all of us.

"My first big assignment was to go to the Soviet Exposition in New York and, after taking all the price tags off the Soviet goods, write in the visitors' book: 'There is no Negro problem in the U.S.S.R.'

"My superiors were so pleased with this job they brought me back to attend the American Exposition in Moscow to write in the visitors' book there: 'What about the Negro in the South?'

"I also was assigned to kick up dust on the exposition floor so the automatic answering machine which answered questions about the United States would break down. I was so successful in this assignment that the Americans had to lay down a new floor.

"But all this was just a warm-up for the Nixon visit.

"My assignment was simple. I had to follow Nixon around on his trip through Russia and just keep asking the same questions over again—what about lynching, unemployment, American bases abroad, and the dirty conditions in the New York subway? I had to switch outfits at every stop. At one place I was a factory worker, at another a peasant, and at several I was just a man in the street.

"But my greatest triumph on the Vice-President's visit was when I dressed up as a meat handler and proudly rejected Nixon's offer of money to buy tickets to the U.S. Exposition. I told him to give the money to the U.S. unemployed, of whom I understood there were 180,000,000.

"For this assignment I was given the Order of Molotov Third Class.

"I would have probably received the Order of Molotov Second Class except for what happened in Poland."

"What happened in Poland?" I asked him.

"After Agitprop's success in Venezuela with Nixon, I was sent to Warsaw to give out tomatoes and eggs to the Polish crowds to throw at the Vice-President. But there seems to be a shortage of eggs and tomatoes in Poland, and the crazy Poles, instead of throwing them, took them home and ate them.

"When Nixon went home I had a few small assignments, such as posing Soviet children in front of American tourists and taking pictures of the deliberate insult of giving candy to weaken our independence and sovereignty. Then I was sent to Vienna for the Communist Youth Festival.

"I'll admit I made a mistake there, but it was a normal one—anyone could have made it. At a giant youth rally I started screaming, 'Why don't they give Paul Robeson a passport so he can leave the United States?' Everyone started taking up the chant until someone realized Paul Robeson had been given a passport and was the guest of honor at the rally.

"No one in Moscow heard about it, and so I was given the most important assignment any Agitprop agent has ever had.

"My assignment was to go to Scotland in connection with President Eisenhower's visit. I was disguised as an unemployed member of the Transport and General Workers' Union, who have gone on record against the H-bomb. In my pocket I carried a membership card in the Nuclear Disarmament Campaign.

"My job was to get struck on the head by President Eisenhower's golf ball. I was out on the course early in the morning, and I did everything to get hit. No matter where I stood, he missed me. Only afterward did I find out the record shows President Eisenhower could not hit anyone with a golf ball.

"I failed in my mission, and now I'm afraid to go home."

I told Alexandrov I felt sorry for him.

He said, "When I went on the assignment they told me they were keeping my wife as hostage, and if I didn't come back, they would kill her. She was driving me crazy anyway, so at least I'm rid of her. I guess every story has a bright side to it."

8. "Bouillabaisse"

Letters I Never Get Around To Answering

Dear Sir,

I am a senior at Sarah Lawrence College and I was wondering if you would be able to tell me what the job opportunities are in Paris at the moment. I was editor of my high school paper and am now writing a column for my college newspaper. I have also done dramatics in college and appeared in school productions of *The Man Who Came to Dinner*, *Dear Ruth*, and three one-act plays by Tennessee Williams.

I would like to work on the European Edition of the *Herald Tribune* as a reporter, but would be willing to start as a secretary or a researcher. I don't speak any French but I've studied Spanish. I understand French is a lot like Spanish. Could you please advise me how I could get a job and how much it would pay. I am enclosing a list of people for references.

I will be finished at Sarah Lawrence in the spring. Could you please advise me if it is difficult to find an apartment in Paris and how much it would cost for a girl to live in Paris.

If I can't get a job on the *Herald Tribune*, would you send me a list of other American business firms in Paris who could use me. I would love to live in Paris and would appreciate hearing from you as soon as possible as I don't want to come over to France without a job.

Sincerely yours,

S. L.

Dear Mr. Buchwald,

The Andorra-American Society would like to have you as their guest speaker for lunch on Feb. 25. We will provide transportation and hotel accommodations.

We don't have a budget for speakers, but I understand you don't charge for speaking. All five members of the Andorra-American Society are ardent readers of the *Herald Tribune* and we're dying to meet you. If Feb. 25 is not acceptable to you, would you please give us a date in March.

Sincerely,

L.Z.

Program Chairman.

Dear Buck,

I guess you'll be surprised hearing from me after all these years, but I just thought I'd sit down and write old Buck a letter. I was in your algebra class at the annex of Jamaica High School, if you remember. Mr. Schmidt was the teacher and, boy, did we have a ball in those days.

I know we didn't hit it off to well, mostly because you were a pretty snotty kid and I had to give you a couple of good beatings before you saw the light, but I say let bygones be bygones (gee, did your nose bleed easily) and your childhood friends are the ones you remember the most.

To get to the point of this letter, a shoe buyer from Gimbels is coming to Paris next month (I'm in the shoe business now), and I told him we grew up together, so he asked me to write you a letter telling you he was coming. I would appreciate it if you would see him and take him and his wife out a couple of nights on your swindle sheet (ha, ha). Perhaps your wife could take his wife shopping.

This account means a lot to me, Buck, and I wouldn't ask you to do this except for the fact we were together at good old Jamaica High.

If your wife needs any shoes wholesale let me know. I don't read your column but I have some friends who do.

Your pal,
Ziggy.

Dear Mr. Buchwald,

When you moved out of my apartment two years ago and I took inventory, I assumed that everything was in order. I have now discovered that the base of the lamp in the living room is broken and the present tenants say it was broken when they moved in. I think in all honesty you should have told me about it.

I would appreciate it if you sent me your check for 12,-450 francs.

Sincerely yours,
Madame H.

Dear Sir,

I am writing a term paper on Napoleon and wood appreciate it if you wood send me all the information you have on the subject. Cood you also send me stamps of

Napolon as part of the paper is to dramatize this grate man and what he did for France. I must have this term paper in by next Friday so I wood appreciate your response as quickly as possible.

Yours truly,
Geoffry Jones,
Farmingdale, Junior High School.

Dear Mr. Buchwald,

Could you please put me in contact with Mr. Paul Getty as I have a sure-fire system of beating the roulette wheel.

If you can make this contact for me, and Mr. Getty is willing to finance me, I will give you 10 per cent of my winnings. I assure you that you will be able to become a rich man. I need $1,000 for the initial investment, but my system cannot lose. Please keep this in confidence as I don't want to be banned from the casinos.

Sincerely yours,
C.K.

Guest Column

(*While I was on vacation I asked Mr. Hebredes Hogenblatt, Minister of Tourism for the tiny principality of Lovlost-by-the-Sea, to tell us about his country.*)

I AM happy to report Lovlost-by-the-Sea has doubled its tourism figures since 1958. Six tourists visited our country this year, as opposed to three last year. This showed a 100 per cent increase in what has now become our third-largest industry, preceded only by smuggling and automobile accidents. To honor the occasion Lovlost has issued a special postage stamp showing a statue of a tourist holding a Thomas Cook bus in one hand and the Paris branch of the American Express in the other.

In order to meet this influx of foreigners, Lovlost has started a major tourist expansion program. For example, Lovlost is offering a 15 per cent reduction in hotel bills for anyone who pays in hard currency. We were able to get this measure through the Finance Ministry because there are no hotels in Lovlost.

The nearest we came to having one was when Conrad Hilton passed through the country on his way to Istanbul. To honor the occasion Lovlost issued a special postage stamp showing a statue of Mr. Hilton's arm waving through the window of a fast-moving train.

But what Lovlost lacks in hotels it makes up in tourist attractions. There is the famed Lying Tower of Pizza. The tower, built in the fifteenth century, fell down the day after it was constructed, and has been lying on the ground ever since.

Then there is the famed Valley of the Lost Echoes. When you shout something into the valley there is no echo.

In the tiny town of Zachimorra you will find one of the best examples of modern stained-glass windows. The town is located next to a coal mine and all the windows in the town are stained by black dust.

Farther north is the scenic whine country, where the people are whining all the time.

In August there is a whine festival. This is not to be confused with the whaling festival, which is held in September in the south. Instead of whining here everyone wails. So if you miss one you can always make the other.

Lovlost is a shopper's paradise. You can get hand-woven hands, hand-painted hands, hand-blocked hands, hand-stitched hands, and hands-across-the-sea hands.

There are also bargains on gloves.

During the months from October to June, Lovlost has a thrift season and tourists can save hundreds of dollars by not going there.

I have only spoken about a few of the many attractions Lovlost has to offer. Being so close to the sea, Lovlost has many first-class fish restaurants where from twelve until two and from seven until nine you can see all kinds of fish eating.

Lovlost has many gastronomic, regional specialties. Among them are Campbell's Tomato Soup, Heinz' Pork and Beans, Hormel's Spam, and Mother O'Hara's Chili Con Carne. Most of it was left over from the war, when the American Army had a food supply depot just outside of the capital.

The people of Lovlost are friendly, kind, considerate, outspoken, outgoing, and out to make a buck.

They hate pretension, and if you pretend you're being overcharged they will become very hurt.

I would like to take this opportunity to invite everyone to my country. You will get a warm welcome, and when the time comes to leave you will not be able to. This is not only because of the affection you will have in your heart for our little country, but also because you'll need an exit visa. Needing tourists like we do, we haven't issued one in ten years.

Economy Drives We Have Known

COMPANIES throughout the world are either in the midst of expanding or in the process of economizing. It depends on what the last financial report looked like. The motion picture companies for the most part are economizing. One major studio has closed down all its European supervisory offices in a wave of economy the likes of which hasn't been seen since the last economy wave.

Since most people are innocent victims of economy drives, I have, as a public service, contacted Mr. Robert Goldbogen, who specializes in studying economy drives and their effect on the economy.

"Mr. Goldbogen, what does an economy drive really mean?"

"It means," Mr. Goldbogen said, "that the president of the company has had to report to the stockholders that the profits are lower than anticipated; there is in fact a loss and he is immediately instigating the necessary measures to turn the tide. As a start, he announces an economy drive will be put in effect. If he's still president after the report he has to follow through on his promise."

"What does he do first?"

"He fires two men, one in the mail room and the elevator boy."

"But who runs the elevator?"

"At a cost of only twenty-five thousand dollars, a self-service elevator is installed."

"That's all?"

"No, it really isn't as economical to fire the mail room

boy as one might think. Someone has to deliver important packages and letters by hand, so a higher-priced employee is sent instead. This employee, not familiar with the city, takes twice as long to do the job as the mail room boy did.

"When the president discovers the firing of the mail room boy and the elevator boy has not solved his problem, he makes further economies."

"How does he do this?"

"Every large company has certain people that they employ just to blame things on. They have to be on the job when things go wrong. Each vice-president might have one chief blame-taker and three assistants. The chief blame-taker distributes the blame among the others. Since there are enough people to spread the blame about, no one gets in trouble. But then the president sends down word to the heads of the departments that they have to cut their staffs and instead of four people, they can only have one."

"The department head naturally keeps the chief blame-taker?"

"Not necessarily. The department head keeps the one who takes the blame the best. The chief blame-taker may be good at dispensing blame, but weak on taking it himself."

"Then the economy problem is settled?"

"On the contrary, this is the most dangerous type of economy there is. Since the head of the department keeps blaming one person for everything that goes wrong, eventually the president asks why the head of the department doesn't fire him? We know the answer. If the head of the department fires him, then he will have to take the blame himself.

"When he takes the blame, he will be fired as well, and pretty soon the president will have to take the blame. Then the stockholders will force *his* resignation. When you start firing people who absorb blame, you're really in a fix."

"What can one do to make sure one is not a victim of an economy cut?"

"Take the bull by the horns, as we say on the back lot in Pamplona. When you smell an economy cut you must immediately go in to see the boss and ask him to let you go.

"Tell him you're expendable, and you feel the company is not getting its money's worth. The boss will immediately smell a rat and decide you're trying to go over to the opposition and you will be kept on the pay roll until hell freezes over.

"Another method of staying on is that as soon as an economy wave is announced the person must demand a raise and a vacation. The boss will figure anyone who would do such a thing at a time like this must be worth a great deal to the firm, and you'll survive the cuts and possibly even get the raise.

"There are other methods. I know one man who owned two cars. One he drove and the other he kept parked in the company parking lot next to the spot reserved for the president's car. No matter what time the president came out, day or night, the man's car was there, and the president assumed he was inside working for Dear Old Inc. Incorporated. It made quite an impression on the president, so much so that when the president had the choice of firing the man or himself, he immediately resigned and the man who owned the car is now president of the company."

Is There a Stock Market?

THERE was a time in the past when nephews used to write their uncles for baseball gloves, ice skates, and hockey sticks. But all this has changed, as I discoverd the other day when I got a letter from my eleven-year-old nephew who was very upset over some advice I had given him.

I take pleasure in publishing my answer to his letter on the off chance that other uncles may be having the same problem.

This was his letter to me.

Dear Uncle Arthur,

You told me to buy Anaconda Copper, and General Dynamics, and Richfield Oil. Since I've bought them they've all gone down. Joel Seligman's grandfather told him to buy land. Nancy Gordon's uncle said she should buy 5 per cent government bonds, and Jimmy Markay's father said the stock market is in for trouble and Jimmy said I should sell my stocks.

Please tell me who is right and why you told me to buy the stocks that went down.

With love,
Eric

This was the reply:

Dear Eric,

Your little friends are wrong. They have been affected by the skepticism of a skeptical age. They think that nothing can be which is not comprehensible to their little minds.

All the stocks I recommended to you were long-term investments. What you are doing is investing in the future of America and the growth potential of the United States. Yes, Eric, there is an Anaconda Copper Company. Sometimes there is a demand for copper and sometimes there isn't. That's what makes the price fluctuate. If your little friends would use more copper instead of telling you what to do with your allowance, they would be doing you a service.

As for investing in the stock market. Alas, how dreary would be the world if there was no stock market. There would be no stockholder meetings, no dividends, no raids. There would be no *Wall Street Journal*, no financial analysts to make tolerable this sad world we live in.

Not believe in the stock market? You might as well not believe in the Republican party. Not believe in dividends? You might as well not believe in the New Haven Railroad.

Eric, instead of your friends telling you to buy 5 per cent government bonds, they should be writing to Washington protesting the unrealistic tight money policies of the present administration that is restricting investment and expansion in some of our key industries, such as copper, dynamics, and oil. Instead of spending all their time criticizing your uncle's advice, they could ask questions, such as how a company can make an honest and fair profit in the face of spiraling wages and inflationary union demands?

Get out of the stock market? I would get out of the Little League first. My advice to you, Eric, is to buy and buy and buy. Let your friends sell short if they want to.

The price of copper is bound to rise, and then you will have the last laugh on them.

No stock investments? Thank heaven, there will always be a stock market. A thousand years from now, ten thousand years, nay, ten times ten thousand years from now, your investment will have compounded, and don't forget, Eric, there is always a chance for bonus dividends.

Your loving,
Uncle Arthur.

P. S. Don't let your friends give you that jazz about Santa Claus taking care of them. There is no Santa Claus. The only thing to believe in is the Dow-Jones averages.

Your loving,
Uncle Arthur.

What Hath El Al Wrought

One always likes to be in on historical events, whether your name is Don Ameche, who invented the telephone, or Spencer Tracy, who invented the electric light bulb.

The other day, out of the clear blue sky a representative of El Al, the Israeli airlines, called me and said, "You have been selected to receive the first air-to-ground telephone call in the history of commercial aviation."

The man explained that El Al Airlines was inaugurating a new service enabling passengers aboard their airliners to call their loved ones in any part of the world by radio-telephone similar to the ones used on ocean-going ships.

It was something new in aviation, he told me, and he said,

since they had to call someone the first time, El Al wanted it to be a newspaperman as it's easier to make history that way.

"You can have a scoop," he promised.

On further questioning I discovered that I wouldn't be the first one to receive such a call. El Al has been experimenting with air-to-ground telephone for almost a year. Some time ago Queen Elizabeth of Belgium called King Baudouin from an El Al plane and spoke to him for five minutes.

"Doesn't that eliminate me as the first person to receive a telephone call from an airplane?" I asked.

"Not really," the man said. "The Queen spoke *unofficially* to King Baudouin. Yours will be the first *official* call. In the record books you will get the credit."

It's the record books that count, and so I agreed to get the first official call and told him to go ahead with the arrangements.

The man telephoned back in two hours and said, "You will be receiving the call at two in the morning."

"Can't you make it earlier?" I asked.

"We want to do it from the middle of the Atlantic and the plane won't be over the middle of the Atlantic until two in the morning."

If you want to be part of history you have to lose a little sleep, so I said all right.

That night I went home and told my wife I was going to get a long-distance call at two in the morning.

"From whom?" she wanted to know.

"I don't know," I said truthfully. "It's from the middle of the Atlantic."

"The middle of the Atlantic at two in the morning?"

"From an airplane. Doesn't everybody?"

She thought about this for a moment.

"I think it's silly," she said.

"Marconi's wife probably said the same thing to him," I retorted.

I made a big pot of coffee, got dressed in a warm bathrobe, and, with a volume of *Lives of Great Inventors*, waited. And waited—and waited. At four o'clock I called long distance and asked the operator if there had been any calls for me.

"Where from?"

"About twenty-five thousand feet over the middle of the Atlantic."

She hung up on me.

At seven o'clock when the call didn't come through I decided El Al had failed and I went to sleep.

I called the El Al man the next afternoon and told him the call hadn't come. There was a pause. Then he said, "Sun spots," and hung up.

But Sunday morning, while I was taking a bath, the phone rang, and I got out of the tub dripping wet to answer it.

A voice on the other end said, "This is Chief Pilot Zvi Tohar calling from El Al Airlines over the middle of the Atlantic. How are you?"

"I'm all wet," I said. "I was taking a bath."

There was a pause and I imagined I was supposed to say something.

"You were supposed to call the other morning."

"I know," he said. "Sun spots."

There was another pause.

"How much does it cost to make a call from an airplane?" I asked, trying to make conversation.

"Between five and ten dollars," he replied.

"Oh," I said.

Another pause. Then to be original I asked, "How's the weather up there?"

"Fine," he said. "Nice and clear."

"Well, it's been nice talking to you." I said.

"Same here," he said.

"Good-by," I said.

"Good-by," he said.

And that was it. One man flying a plane and the other man taking a bath can now talk to each other by telephone. Will scientific wonders never cease?

Death to Small Cars

I RECEIVED an interesting request from a public relations feller apparently representing one of the major automobile companies. Since it wasn't marked confidential, I can tell you about it.

The feller said his company was putting out a special supplement in *The New York Times* next month in the United States, to introduce their new line of automobiles, particularly their small car.

The feller writes: "We would like to point up some of the advantages of the American small car, by dwelling on the disadvantages of the European small car . . . The idea would be for Buchwald to write about the dubious joys of owning a European small car, probably not even mentioning American small cars, but leaving the implication that European small cars are: (1) Much too small. (2) Not designed for the human being, particularly on long trips. (3) Often difficult to repair, especially the exotic makes, and so on.

"Payment for regular Buchwald-length column would be $1,500. Article must be in by the end of August."

Now this is the best offer I've had in weeks. I could use fifteen hundred dollars in the worst way, particularly since I have my heart set on buying a French-made Simca, which, by coincidence comes to about the offered fee.

The problem is not whether I should do the article or not, but what I can say to leave the implication this American company wants.

As a starter, I asked friends of mine what they didn't like about their European cars.

One man said, "You get too many miles to the gallon. I rarely get to stop at a service station."

"Is that bad?"

"Well, a fellow likes to go to a rest-room *once in a while*."

Another friend said, "The worst thing about owning a small European car is that it's much too small, and you can always find a parking place."

"What's wrong with that?"

"I own a parking lot. It's killing my business."

Still another friend complained about the seating.

"My European small car is too big. It has room for myself, a wife, and three children."

"Well, what's wrong with that?"

"I'm not married."

Each person I talked to was bitter about the small car. One man I knew casually complained, "If you own a small car, you get through traffic twice as fast as with a big car. Since I bought my small car, I'm home for dinner at seven o'clock instead of eight."

"What's wrong with that?"

"I can't stand my wife's cooking."

Another man said his only objection to the European small car was that his kids kept lifting it off the driveway and putting it on his lawn so they could play handball against the garage door.

One man said, "The European small car is okay on the highway but it is hell when you're trying to see a drive-in movie, particularly if you have to park in the back row."

"Do you think small cars should get into movie drive-ins for half price?" I asked him.

"Yes and no. They tried it once near Cannes, but then they wouldn't let us in when the picture was advertised "For Adults Only."

I haven't had time to do too much research on the column, but it's coming along fine and I hope to have the copy in by the end of August like the feller said.

It's about time somebody took off after these little European small cars, and this American automobile company really has a good idea. Of course, there are some people who will say why doesn't this American automobile company pick on somebody its own size?

But they're just people who don't understand big business, or else they're people who don't have a chance to pick up an easy fifteen hundred for seven hundred words.

I don't care what they say—a man's got to live and if I don't write the article, somebody else sure as hell will.

A Cat Protests

I WENT to see the film *Cat on a Hot Tin Roof* and it got me to thinking. If you haven't seen the picture you won't know what I was thinking about.

Briefly, it's the story of a cat on a hot tin roof (Elizabeth Taylor), who is constantly being rebuffed in her slip by her athletically minded husband (Paul Newman).

The father, who is known as Big Daddy (Burl Ives), owns twenty-eight thousand acres of the richest farmland in the area plus four million dollars. He's going to die, but Mr. Newman doesn't want either the land or the money. Since Mr. Newman doesn't want Miss Taylor either, the problem of the picture is just what the hell he does want.

He drinks about a bottle of whisky a scene, so we know he likes whisky, but, as the picture progresses, we discover whisky is just a substitute for something else.

In the end we find all he ever wanted was Big Daddy to love him.

Well, that's about the picture in a nutshell. What got me to thinking is what damage this picture could do American men abroad. It makes us look pretty bad to reject Miss Taylor right off the bat and to keep rejecting her throughout the film. But to throw away the inheritance as well, just because his father doesn't love him, really puts a burden

on the imaginations of people we are trying to sell the American way of life to.

It isn't healthy for anybody.

The problem is how to explain to the French, for example, that there really aren't three young American men in America, including Mr. Newman, who would throw Elizabeth Taylor out of their bedrooms. It isn't done, not even in the United States. And as for kissing away four million dollars and twenty-eight thousand acres of the best farmland in Mississippi because his father didn't give him anything but money when he was a kid—well, there may be people like that in America, but they never lived in my neighborhood.

My problem was just the opposite. My father loved me, but he didn't give me any money. Instead of cars and gifts, he showered me with affection. It got me nowhere, so I started drinking, but *I* knew what I was drinking about.

As for Miss Taylor, she was in Hollywood making *National Velvet*, and Louis B. Mayer wouldn't let me get near her anyway. That's the way it was with most American kids. But how are you going to get over *that* message to the French?

Anyone who has seen any French pictures lately knows how ridiculous it is for them to accept the situation of *Cat on a Hot Tin Roof*.

There is a French film in Paris which has been playing for a long time to capacity crowds in three theaters. It's called *Les Amants* (*The Lovers*), and it is the story of a beautiful young married woman who is going to spend the week-end with her husband *and* her lover at their country home. Driving down to the home, her car breaks down and she is given a lift by a handsome student. He is invited by the husband to spend the week-end, much to the chagrin of the lover.

During the night the wife and the student meet in the woods and fall in love.

This love scene and the following ones take up most of the picture. In the morning the wife decides to leave with the student.

Her original lover wants to slug the student, but a friend points out he isn't the husband and has no rights. The husband, a newspaper editor (though this isn't true of all French newspaper editors), doesn't seem to care. The picture ends with the student and wife driving off into the sunrise.

Now this is a true slice of French life, and it isn't hard for any American to believe it. Then why, I keep asking myself, can't the Americans show a true slice of American life?

When Paul Newman turns his back on Elizabeth Taylor he does a disservice to all of us. And I believe the rest of us cats should not take it lying down!

How To Speak Italian

IF YOU can walk, you can dance. If you can thrash your hands, you can speak Italian. The farther south you go in Italy, the more people use their arms and hands to express themselves. In some parts of the country, such as Rome, the use of the hands is the most important part of the language, and the voice is only used to emphasize a point.

As a public service, we are printing the necessary phrases one needs in Rome. If you learn these phrases you won't have any chance of being misunderstood.

The first thing to learn in Italian is "I am hungry."

You say this by taking your right hand, fingers out, palm down, and slowly drawing it out in a circle coming back to your stomach. This is pure Italian. If you want to use slang, rub both hands against the stomach, and groan.

You arrive at the railroad station, and you have no money to tip the porter. You take the thumb and index finger of the right hand and bend the other fingers. Then make a circular movement, using only your wrist. It means you don't have it.

The porter will then take his thumb and place it behind his upper incisors and push it out fast. This means in Italian, "Drop Dead."

It is then your turn to say, "I don't care." You do this by sticking your chin out, pursing your lower lip, and with fingers in and straight, caress your neck up to your chin several times.

If the porter raises his hand and makes a fist with it, it means he wants to hit you. The best thing to do is place your right hand in your pocket and take out any foreign currency you have, and hold it out. The fist will open automatically, and the discussion will end on a happy note.

Rome is a city of beautiful women, and Italian men are constantly expressing their delight in them. In the taxi, when the driver sees a beautiful woman, he will take both hands off the wheel. With his left hand he'll point out the monument, and with his right he will join his thumb and index finger and bring it up to his cheek, twisting it from right to left in a slow motion.

If you agree she is indeed beautiful, you make a circle with your right thumb and index finger and kiss them. For extra emphasis you can purse your lips and roll your eyes.

If, on the other hand, you think she's only so-so, put your right hand straight out, fingers closed, palm down, and slowly move the hand from left to right.

The taxi driver will then probably bring his shoulders up to his neck, push his chest forward, and stick both hands out with palms up. This means, "What do you want from me?"

At this juncture you will almost hit a bus. The bus driver will stick his head and right hand out the window and, bunching his fingers together facing up, will shake them back and forth. This translates into English as, "What are you doing?"

The taxi driver will then stick out his fingers in the same manner, but move them faster. He is answering by saying, "What the hell do you think I'm doing?"

The drivers in the back who are stopped will start waving their arms, and the policeman on the corner will take both his hands, place the palms together, and move them back and forth against his chest. He is saying, "Please, please, don't argue in the middle of the street."

The taxi driver is so wrought up by now that he has run out of things to say, so he lifts his hand to his mouth and starts biting his index finger. This translates literally from the Italian, "Words fail me."

The bus driver then takes his thumb and draws it downward along his cheek, which means, "I'll get you if it takes me ten years."

The policeman blows his whistle in anger, and the bus moves off. The taxi driver turns to you, and with both index fingers sticking out, he brings them slowly together. This means that as far as the taxi driver is concerned the policeman and the bus driver are conspiring together.

If you want to say, "Shut up," hold both the taxi driver's hands so he can't move them.

There are of course many other expressions in the past, future, and pluperfect tenses, but if you learn those in the present you can get by.

I've been in Rome for a week and ever since I got my wrist limbered up by eating pasta I haven't had to open my mouth (a neat trick in itself).

You really get to know the people when you speak their language.

Ski Resorting, The Sport of

SKI resorting, not to be confused with skiing at a resort, is one of the most popular pastimes in winter sports today. Most ski resorting takes place on the rocky bluffs or the intimate pistes of hotel lobbies and bars in snowy areas.

Since there is so much more interest in ski resorting than there is in resort skiing, I have borrowed the services of Aspen Piznair, the 1958 Olympic Ski Resort Champion, who now has a clinic at St. Moritz for people who are going downhill without any visible means of support.

Mr. Piznair answered questions about ski resorting and techniques in my column:

Problem: I am a beginner at ski resorting and wish to improve myself. But I find in the lobby of the Palace Hotel that so many of the women are more advanced than I am that when I try to sideslip I always fall on my face. How can I compete against all the ice in the lobby? I'm only a secretary. S. L.

Answer: Ski resorting takes confidence. The secret of success is not in how much ice there is in the lobby but how much body control you use. Hip swinging and body rotation are the keys to successful ski resorting. Stretch pants and a tight sweater can also be of help. Don't sit down but keep moving. Control the drift of your turn by maintaining an upright relaxed body position. In no time at all you will be on equal footing with the more experienced ski resorters and your shorthand days will be over.

Problem: I hate skiing, have always hated it, ever since my father beat me with a ski pole. But I like hot chocolate. (My mother used to give me hot chocolate after my father beat me.) Do you know of any place I can get hot chocolate outside of a ski resort? R. B.

Answer: No.

Problem: I just bought a new pair of ski boots with steel stays and twist-reinforced quarter and full-length counters. I paid fifty-two dollars for them. Every afternoon my husband insists we go for a walk, but I don't want to because I'll get snow on them. Am I being unreasonable? F. G.

Answer: Absolutely not; it's your husband who is unreasonable. Wearing ski boots in the snow is the worst thing that you can do with them. Good ski boots are hard to come by and should only be used for dancing or bowling. If your husband insists on taking walks, make him buy you a pair of galoshes.

Problem: The other day a man in the lobby of the Suvretta House asked me to write something on his cast. I don't know him very well, and I was at a loss as to what to say. I told him I'd think about it. Each day he keeps bothering me and says he is saving a good place for me just below his knee. What can I write? Miss S. P.

Answer: Writing on a cast is a tricky business, particularly when you're not well acquainted with the leg. "I'd like to fall for you," or "The next time you're casting, give me a break," or "Set 'em up in the other alley," are all acceptable. Try to avoid sentimentality and don't put anything in writing that you'll be sorry for later. If you like the person, you could put a return address on the shin.

Problem: I have been the photographer at the Corviglia Ski Club for twenty-five years. I am seventy-three years old. There is a rule in the club that I am not permitted to sit down. Do you think this is right? Dr. S.

Answer: Yes, we do. As the club photographer, you have no right to sit down with the guests, and, after all, you're only seventy-three years old and should be able to stand on your own two feet. If we let you sit down, then the headwaiter would want to sit down, and the ski instructors would want to sit down, and pretty soon no one would be on their toes. Perhaps on your eightieth birthday we'll let you *lean* against a wall, but sitting in a chair is out of the question.

Problem: Elsa Maxwell is in St. Moritz now and she's giving a big dinner party to which I haven't been invited. How can I have a good time if I'm not invited to her party?

Answer: Try breaking your arm on the bobsled run.

This book was set in

Janson and Deepdene types by

The Haddon Craftsmen.

It was printed at

the press of The World Publishing Company.